Derek Robinson's

Best Green Walks in BRISTOL

AND WHERE TO PARK SO YOU CAN ENJOY THEM

WESTCOUNTRY
—BOOKS—

First published in 1994
by Westcountry Books

© Derek Robinson

ISBN 1 898386 09 9

British Library Cataloguing-in-Publication Data
CIP data for this book is available from the British Library.

Westcountry Books
Halsgrove House
Lower Moor Way
Tiverton
Devon EX16 6SS

Tel: 01884 243242
Fax: 01884 243325

Typeset and printed in Great Britain
by Longdunn Press, Bristol.

Cover illustration: Painted by Quentin Williams,
showing part of the Frome Valley Walk.

CONTENTS

ABOUT THE WALKS

If you live in Bristol, and you want to go for a walk in green countryside, the good news is that you needn't drive to the Cotswolds , the Mendips, or the Brontë country.

A dozen walks are waiting for you, all in Bristol (or on its edge), and all different. They're rich in trees and birds, cliffs and gorges, meadows and streams.

This book tells you where they are, how to find them, and — most important of all — where you can park. (No point in setting out if you can't park when you get there.)

It also tells you what sort of walk it is — long or short, muddy or dry, rugged or easy. So you'll know what to wear, and how much time to allow. Also whether or not it's a good idea to take small children and/or elderly relatives.

I know these walks, because I've walked them all — every inch, many times and in every weather. And to my amazement I've often been the only walker in sight — even on a fine summer evening. Presumably the rest of Bristol was indoors, watching TV. So if you want to enjoy the peace and beauty of nature (trees and stuff), it's out there waiting, believe me.

And not far off, either. Most walks are inside the city, a few are on the fringe. And best of all, they're free (including parking). These walks are in town — but they're country walks, all the same.

Blaise Castle Estate

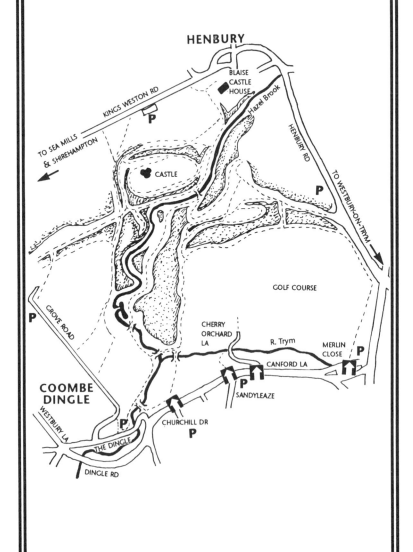

BLAISE CASTLE ESTATE, KINGSWESTON DOWN, AND PENPOLE WOODS

This is my favourite. From end to end it must be at least three miles. How many people know they can take a there-and-back walk in Bristol for six miles in unbroken, beautiful woods and parkland, without once having to set foot on a road?

Or you can choose a chunk of it. Blaise Castle has many short walks (grassland, hill, or gorge). Kingsweston Down is just that: a long mile of rolling downland, flanked with woods. It leads westward to the old Kingsweston Estate and Penpole Woods: half a mile of tall timber that narrows to a high point, overlooking the Severn Estuary. Each part has its charms. Put them all together and you have an unbroken green walk on well-marked trails all the way from Henbury to Avonmouth.

BLAISE CASTLE ESTATE

Parking

You can get into the Estate from the north (Kings Weston Road) or the east (Henbury Road) or the south (Canford Lane/The Dingle).

Parking on the North Side

Kings Weston Road (B4057) runs from Henbury village westward towards Sea Mills and Shirehampton. At the edge of the village it passes Blaise Castle House. Two hundred yards further on is a large car-park (100 spaces). If it's full, backtrack and turn left down Hallen Road: you might find room in Castle Close or Hallen Close. Alternatively, drive on towards Shirehampton and take the first turning right, Long Cross. Plenty of parking space here. You can get into the Estate by crossing Kings Weston Road. There are public toilets near the large car-park.

Parking on the East Side

Henbury Hill which becomes Henbury Road connects Westbury-on-Trym with Henbury village. Assume you're coming from Westbury. Just over the brow of the hill, Henbury Road suddenly widens and creates half-a-dozen parking spaces on the left, near the driveway entrance to the Estate. Alternatively, drive on a short way and turn right into Didsbury Close or Arnall Drive.

Parking on the South Side

South of Blaise Castle Estate lie Henbury golf course and the River Trym. South of this is Canford Lane — the main road between Westbury-on-Trym and Sea Mills/Coombe Dingle. There are five ways into Blaise Castle from Canford Lane or The Dingle. All are public footpaths. Three go through the golf course. Note: there is no public footpath across the golf course. Except where signposted differently, your path is around the edge. Often it is through the woods, which — let's face it — is probably the safest place to be, with all those mis-hit golf balls flying about.

(1) At the Westbury end of Canford Lane, look for a colony of prefabs, called Merlin Close. To its left a public footpath follows

the golf club boundary fence. After 50 yards, a stile lets you onto the course; or you can walk on up the path and join it at a higher point. To get to Blaise Castle you'll have to walk the length of the course. Parking is usually easy near Merlin Close.

(2) Further along Canford Lane is what looks like someone's private driveway, between numbers 251 and 253, signposted 'Cherry Orchards'. In fact this is a genuine single track lane. Don't even think of parking on it. Best place to park is in Sandyleaze, across Canford Lane.

Cherry Orchards Lane dips down to make a bridge over the Trym. From here you can take the footpath upstream or downstream. Or you can cross the bridge and climb the steep and winding lane, past some handsome old houses, until it looks as if you've reached a dead end, but at the last minute you're saved by a public footpath on your right. This gets narrower and rockier as it climbs, squeezed between barbed wire and brambles, but it's worth the effort because it delivers you to the edge of the 17th hole of the golf course (the par 3 'Oak Tree', heavily guarded by bunkers). Turn left and walk through the trees, and behind the driving green you'll see a wall. Go and look over it. Yawning beyond and below is the great Beech Cathedral of Blaise Castle.

(3) Near Cherry Orchards Lane is a signposted public footpath beside 263 Canford Lane. Here again the best place to park is in Sandyleaze. The path hugs the ends of several suburban gardens, trips over a few enormous fox-holes, and stumbles down to meet the lane at the bridge.

(4) The next public footpath is signposted to Blaise Castle. It's opposite Churchill Close (a cul-de-sac off Canford Lane) which is the best place to park. Follow the sign into a small but crowded housing estate and another sign on the left

points you down some steep steps. You emerge in a little meadow where the Trym flows into Hazel Brook (or vice versa). You can turn right and follow the Trym up to the golf course, or go straight ahead and follow Hazel Brook upstream into the Estate.

(5) The Dingle is where Blaise Castle Estate starts to run out. Here there is a gravelled car-park (20 spaces). You can drive to it from the downhill turn-off at the far end of Canford Lane — look for a sign saying STEEP HILL 1:8. Or you can take the road called The Dingle, a turning off Westbury Lane where it joins Sylvan Way. Follow The Dingle down to the river and you'll see the car-park. From here, all of Blaise Castle and Kingsweston Down is yours for the taking.

Short Walk in Blaise: The Castle, Lover's Leap and the Giant's Footprint

Assuming you parked in the big car-park on Kings Weston Road, the splendid huge square building to your left is Blaise Castle House. (More about that later.) The actual Blaise Castle is ahead of you, on top of that wooded hill. Climb straight up the hill or take any of the trails that wind around it, work your way to the summit and you'll find the Castle.

Considering it's been there for over 200 years, and often sadly neglected, the Castle's in pretty good nick. It's a curious triangular design, with three round towers of odd heights: like an early Gothic condiment set. But although it's a sham castle, it's a real sham, because it was built to be used as a summer house. It had a kitchen downstairs, a big drawing room upstairs, stained glass windows, carved panelling, suits of armour, and similar fake medieval bric-à-brac. The well-to-do enjoyed playing at Camelot in those days. The owner actually installed six cannon on the top tower.

The hilltop itself has a long history of occupation. The Romans built a temple on it, and before that there was an Iron Age fort — look hard and you might see some evidence. Later there was a medieval chapel dedicated to St Blasius, patron saint of wool-combers, whose name became Blaise.

From the clearing it's only a few yards to the railings guarding Lover's Leap. (That is where the map puts the apostrophe, so I suppose the lover plunged to his/her doom all alone, since a suicide pact would have resulted in Lovers' Leap.) The undergrowth beyond the railings is so thick that any lover would have to perform a leap of Olympic dimensions in order to clear it, and so the view is a bit limited, but you can see two great limestone crags projecting from the opposite side of the Gorge. These are the wings of Goram's Chair. They match the cliff that's under your feet, which gives your imagination something to work on. And on the far distant horizon is Dundry Hill.

Follow the path to the left and eventually it leads back to the lawns in front of Blaise Castle House. About 50 yards down the path from Lover's Leap is a massive bench that marks a marvellous viewpoint. You look out over much of the Gorge and the valley at its rugged best, as far down as Coombe Dingle. Far better than Lover's Leap, in my opinion.

Walk another 100 yards and just before the path joins the main track, watch out for a wide outcrop of white limestone on your left. This is known as Goram's Footprint. If Goram's feet looked anything like this, he had serious need of a good chiropodist.

The truth is it's part of a limestone pavement — quite rare in the south of England. Centuries of erosion have created these curious marks in the stone. Some look like big keyholes.

Short Walk in Blaise: Echo Gate and the Iron Age Fort

Starting from the Kings Weston Road car-park, skirt the right hand side of Castle Hill and you'll find the path narrows and forms a bottleneck, with woodland rising on both sides. Take the path on the right. It climbs by means of steps to a kissing gate at the top.

This is Echo Gate. Face the Castle and shout, and your voice should bounce back. This doesn't work very well in winter, and even in summer you may have to experiment at different points on the steps. When I was a boy the echo was always clear and word-perfect, but nothing's made to last nowadays.

As you climb, look out for two stone boundary markers. They separate Blaise Castle Estate from Kingsweston Estate. The initials JSH identify John Scandrett Harford, for whom Blaise House was built 200 years ago; on the reverse, RJM (and I'm guessing here) stands for one of the Miles family, who owned Kingsweston at about the same time.

Beyond Echo Gate is Kingsweston Down. A few yards away the wall of an Iron Age fort crosses the Down. The fort had four walls but the hillside gave good protection on the other three sides, whereas the open Down was obviously more vulnerable to attack, so the wall-and-ditch defence had to be stronger here.

(Now: if you want to see something of the Gorge, cross the end of the Down and enter the trees, where you'll soon find paths that work their way down to the stream. Alternatively, go back down Echo Gate steps to the foot of Castle Hill. A path to the right, signposted Coombe Dingle, takes you down. Main tracks alongside Hazel Brook lead back to the House.)

After the fort, it's an easy stroll along the Down for as far as you like; then back the way you came, pausing for another yodel at Echo Gate.

Short Walk in Blaise: The Mill, Timber Lodge, The Royals

Follow the driveway from Blaise Castle House across the lawns and down through the Gorge to the bridge over the stream, which is correctly called Hazel Brook. This drive is really a road. It was built for the Harford family by Humphrey Repton, a landscape architect, so that they could have the thrill of getting into their carriage and plunging into the depths of the Gorge, after which they de-plunged up the other side. Hard work for the horses.

Near the bridge is Stratford Mill. Rich Americans are not the only people to dismantle and re-erect old buildings. Until 1952 Stratford Mill was at West Harptree in Somerset, where it had been used to grind barley on the river Chew for 200 years. Then came Chew Magna Reservoir, and the mill was taken to bits and put together again here.

If you don't fancy the climb you see ahead of you, follow the waterside path upstream on the mill side (not the opposite side) and it's an easy walk to The Royals.

If you're rugged enough for the uphill road, be sure to pause on the way and admire the Gorge. It's a miniature version of the Avon Gorge — with one big difference. It was made by the stream, whereas the Avon Gorge was not made by the Avon. Well ... I suppose there was probably a bit of a split here first, half a million years ago, which Hazel Brook got to work on and eroded until it made the spectacular defile you see today.

At the second hairpin bend, take a look at the Woodland Lodge, another of Humphrey Repton's bright ideas. He thought it would be nice if the Harfords, when they wandered over to their windows at Blaise Castle House, could see a gentle plume of smoke emerging from a quaint little cottage on the far side of their valley. What the woodman thought of this, history does not record.

After the next hairpin you're nearly at the top, which is marked by the Timber Lodge. It's been lived in since 1840, so it must be comfortable. Splendid thatch, and the timbering is calculated to make Walt Disney eat his heart out.

From here, turn left and take the steps down through the trees to The Royals, an enormous meadow where, if my guess is right, the Harford cows grazed right royally in order to produce top-quality cream, butter and cheese. Notice the pond in the middle, where the cows drank, and the big trees dotted about, where they found shade in summer.

Head for Henbury church (that's where the path is going, anyway) and cross the stream by bridge and tunnel to the churchyard; then turn left and it's just a hop and a skip to Blaise Castle House. But don't hurry past the church. St Mary's is a fine example of strong and simple church design: no buttresses to prop up the tower, which is probably thirteenth century. The south and north doors are late Norman, and so are the huge pillars in the nave. Why such a big church for a little village? Well, you have to remember that Westbury-on-Trym was an important place long before Bristol existed. It had a Benedictine monastery as long ago as 803; maybe earlier. And in 1093 the Bishop of Worcester (whose diocese included Westbury) gave the church of St Mary to the Benedictine monks as an endowment. So you're looking at a bit of religious history that was well established when Bristol was only a couple of shacks and a scruffy pub.

If you can stand some more history, look for the tombstone of Scipio Africanus, a negro servant of the Earl of Suffolk. He died in 1720, aged 18. Negro graves of this period are rare in Britain because (contrary to popular belief) negro servants were rare, and slaves even rarer. Some Bristolians suffer from the delusion that slaves were auctioned on Blackboy Hill. Not so. The slave trade went from Africa to the West Indies or America, and that's where the auctions took place.

Short Walk in Blaise: Henbury Lodge, Rhododendron Walk and Beech Cathedral

Assuming you parked on or near Henbury Road, take the driveway into Blaise woods, past Henbury Lodge, to Timber Lodge. Follow the path that forks left and climbs. At the right time of year you'll see masses of rhododendrons in bloom. (The Victorians discovered them in the East and were infatuated with them.) Soon you get glimpses on your right of the Gorge, tumbling down to Hazel Brook. Then you reach Goram's Chair, a pair of limestone crags that project to give you a fine view of the rocky heights on the opposite side. The next bend reveals another great sight: a grove of magnificent beech trees, dominating the whole hillside. Their trunks are so straight, tall and clean-cut that they well deserve the title of Beech Cathedral.

   You can go back through the woods at the edge of the golf course (more rhododendrons) or simply return the way you came. Alternatively, for a bit more exercise, carry on past the beeches, climb down to the river, follow it upstream, and turn right at the bridge for the steep climb up to Timber Lodge and Henbury Lodge.

Long Walks in Blaise

These are simply combinations of the short walks. Starting at Coombe Dingle you can walk beside the brook all the way to Stratford Mill and up to Blaise Castle House, and then return via Blaise Castle and Echo Gate. Or you can turn right at Stratford Mill, past Woodman's Cottage to Timber Lodge, then down into The Royals and through the churchyard to the House.

Starting from Blaise Castle House you can walk to Coombe Dingle via the easy riverside route (and back again); or you can stretch your legs a bit and go via the Castle, Echo Gate, and the path down through the woods, opposite Beech Cathedral. After that, if you're really ambitious, cross Hazel Brook, climb up through the beeches and take Rhododendron Walk to The Royals. Or start at Henbury Lodge and do Rhodo Walk and Beech Cathedral, then down and up to Echo Gate, the Castle, the House, the churchyard and The Royals. That should give you an appetite for tea.

KINGSWESTON DOWN

Kingsweston Down stretches from Echo Gate to the iron bridge that spans the cut made by Kings Weston Road as it leaves Sea Mills and heads into Lawrence Weston. But beyond the bridge there is still much of Kingsweston Estate to come, and as this includes the Big House, it's well worth seeing.

Parking

The large car-park off Kings Weston Road near Blaise Castle House puts you near Echo Gate and the Down. Or, to get on the Down about half way along it, there's an entry from Sea Mills. At the bottom of Westbury Lane, turn into The Dingle, then left into Grove Road and drive to the very top where it meets the woods. You can usually park here. A very stony track goes up to the Down. Another way in is at

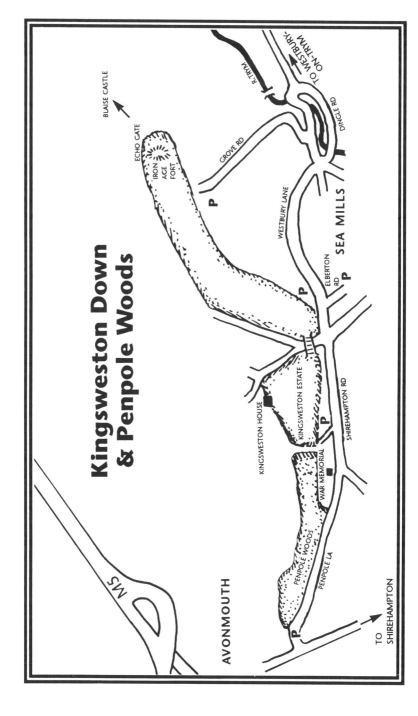

Kingsweston Down & Penpole Woods

BLAISE CASTLE

ECHO GATE

IRON AGE FORT

R-TRYM

TO WESTBURY-ON-TRYM

GROVE RD

DINGLE RD

WESTBURY LANE

ELBERTON RD

SEA MILLS

KINGSWESTON HOUSE

KINGSWESTON ESTATE

SHIREHAMPTON RD

WAR MEMORIAL

PENPOLE WOODS

PENPOLE LA

AVONMOUTH

M5

TO SHIREHAMPTON

the top left hand corner of Sea Mills, where Westbury Lane meets Shirehampton Road. Park either in Westbury Lane or Elberton Road, a side street. It used to be possible to walk up through the woods via a gate at the corner of Westbury Lane, but the last time I tried it the path was clogged with fallen trees and the bridle path was a bog. You're better off using the hard track up to the iron bridge; then turn right.

The Walk

The Down is unique in Bristol: a mile of unbroken, rolling grassland, flanked on each side by wide belts of trees that keep all houses at bay. With nothing to overlook it, the Down is spacious and quiet. The grass is never mown: small boys and large dogs can lose themselves in the prairie. Butterflies abound in summer. Birds abound all year long, and a walk on the Down in the evening is a free concert. The woods on either side contain good paths that run parallel with the Down, so you can walk out through the trees and return on the grass, or vice versa.

Apart from the Iron Age fort near Echo Gate at one end, and the tree-covered foundations of a lost windmill near the other, there's nothing spectacular to look at, but then the Down is made for peace and tranquillity. However, opposite the TV mast is a scene of devastation, or what's left of it. Here the great gale of 1990 came roaring up the Severn, fell upon a fine stand of tall trees, and smashed them over like skittles. You can still see some of the mighty carcasses and their giant roots. Unfortunately you can also see the smokestacks of Severnside, through the gap.

Beside the TV mast is a quarry, unused for many a decade. Its upper and smaller end is rapidly filling with young trees. This makes it a magnet for birds. Enter quietly and you might see something rare and special. The path is on the opposite side to the TV mast. Watch your step.

Next stop is the iron bridge over the stone canyon of Kings Weston Road. Beyond it, a splendid panoramic view suddenly opens up, showing the long sweep of the Horseshoe Bend that the Avon takes from Shirehampton up to the beginning of the Gorge. On a very clear day you can see a tiny bit of the Clifton Suspension Bridge. The foreground is a handsome piece of National Trust land, Shirehampton Park, home to a lot of American soldiers in World War Two; I could show you the holes where they dug slit trenches as punishment drill. Across the Avon are the lush green fields of what once was (and may well be again) Somerset. To the left is Sea Mills, which has the distinction of being the birthplace not only of Robin Cousins but also of me.

The path ahead is obvious, but I suggest you climb through the hole in the wall on your right. Prowl about and you'll find, again on your right, the remains of a fake Classical bit of nonsense that used to be full of fake Classical statues looking down the long tree-lined drive to Kingsweston House, now occupied by Avon and Somerset Police. Stroll down this drive, and a hundred yards from the House you'll see the beginnings of what was obviously going to be another impressive pile if only the builders hadn't stopped when the walls were only five feet high. Now it's covered by ivy and brambles. I'm told that QEH School would have moved here if Hitler hadn't started World War Two. (Instead, QEH remains beneath its brooding battlements, glowering down the longest flight of steps in Berkeley Place.)

Back to the top of the drive. The path runs parallel to the wall, between lines of some truly massive oaks and cypresses. From time to time you'll see slabs of ancient concrete slowly vanishing under moss and lichen. These are all that remains of scores of Nissen huts: this was an army camp in the war, and afterwards the home of an army of mainly Irish labourers who built the Brabazon runway. (If that means nothing to you, ask your grandad.)

Soon you begin to get fine views of Kingsweston House. Take a good look. It was designed by one of the greatest English architects of his time, Sir John Vanbrugh, about 1710, when Clifton regarded itself as a village outside Bristol, when convicted robbers got hanged on Durdham Down, and when Kingsweston was literally a country house. (There was a Big House here before that: William III stayed at Kingsweston in 1690, the guest of its owner, Sir Robert Southwell, Secretary of State for Ireland.)

This isn't the most graceful of Vanbrugh's efforts, but it's certainly strong. Some might say monumental. The windows (very broad, very severe) and the huge pilasters in the middle are eighteenth-century macho. Most dominant of all is the set of six whacking great chimney-stacks, all linked by arches and all completely useless. Vanbrugh put them on because he thought the roof needed a gentrified-fortified look on top. During World War Two, the army had the place. The story I heard was that they were practising with explosives, and next thing, all the chimneys came down. That's why the ones you see look newer than the rest of the building.

PENPOLE WOODS

Parking

Halfway along Shirehampton Road, where it runs straight and level above the golf course, a dirt track turns off towards Kingsweston.

This gives parking space for a dozen cars. The track goes on to lead into Penpole Woods. The other place to park is along Penpole Lane, which turns off Shirehampton Road at the war memorial. You can drive to the end of Penpole Point: usually plenty of space there.

The Walk

This is a short walk: Penpole Woods are only half a mile long. There are two main paths. If you walk down from the iron bridge, one path leads into a short avenue of redwoods, skirts the cricket ground and never gets far from Penpole Lane. The lower path is better. Follow the driveway towards Kingsweston House until you see lumps of masonry at the roadside (more leftovers from the QEH foundations) and the path is on your left.

Penpole is on a surprisingly steep slope, and this makes its big trees even more dramatic. Nevertheless, the walking is easy because the paths are broad and level, and they all end up at the same place: Penpole Point. Nothing remains of the lodge that marked the Estate boundary except some broken-down wall. Nearby is a charming circular seat with a cast-iron basketweave design around a stone pillar. Carry on to the bitter end of the path and you can sit on a bench and stare at Avonmouth docks, the Severn and Wales. It's all a long way from the thatched quaintnesses of Blaise Castle Estate.

The attraction of Penpole Woods is that it's been left to grow as it likes. The gale damage hasn't been tidied up: some big beeches still stand with their upper halves snapped like pencils. On the other hand, the further you walk into the woods, the nearer Shirehampton, Avonmouth and the M5 become: the litter and noise are inescapable. But the squirrels don't seem to mind. I saw six in one tree on a winter's afternoon. And the sunsets over the Severn can be colourful, too.

A Small Bonus: The Dingle
to Sea Mills Harbour

Blaise Castle Estate stops (or starts) at The Dingle, but the Trym still has the best part of a mile to flow before it reaches the Avon, and that mile makes a green and pleasant walk. The path goes through woodland as far as the big white road bridge just beyond the foot of Westbury Lane and Sylvan Way; here, steps lead down from the bridge. Then the valley widens to make a lush green meadow for a couple of hundred yards, until the path becomes a stony track that crosses the Trym at the very spot where there once stood a mill. The ruins were still quite big when I was a boy, and you could clearly recognise the pond that kept a head of water for the mill wheel. (Presumably this was what gave Sea Mills half its name — how the 'Sea' bit fits in, nobody has ever explained to me.)

The track emerges on Shirehampton Road, next to the Mill House pub. You then have to cross the main road and pick up the path on the left of the Trym, after which it's a straightforward stroll, ending underneath the Portway at Sea Mills harbour. Here there are public toilets. (This stretch used to be a swamp, especially at spring tides, but now that it's been reclaimed and the tides are held back, it's all good parkland.)

There's not much doubt that the Romans dammed the Trym to make a floating harbour at Sea Mills (which they called Abonae), because they needed a ferry link and a supply base for their operations in South Wales — which the 2nd Augustan Legion was busily conquering by the second century A.D. — and the mouth of the Trym offered the best anchorage below the Avon Gorge. Abonae was more than a harbour; it was a small town. The Romans built quays, warehouses, streets, houses, a temple, a cemetery, and road links with Bath and Gloucester. For two or three

16

hundred years Abonae flourished. Then Rome abandoned Britain and that was the end of the town.

The massive stone walls rising from the mud are still locally called the Roman Harbour — which they are definitely not. Perhaps they stand on Roman foundations, but the harbour walls you can see were built about 250 years ago by a Bristol whaling company. Ships towed the whales all the way from Greenland, and the butchering was done at Sea Mills because the stench was too much for Bristolians to stomach. Sea Mills didn't turn out to be the ideal spot either, and the firm soon went bust.

Blaise Castle House

John Scandrett Harford was a Quaker and a banker, and it shows, both ways. When he had Blaise Castle House built, 200 years ago, the design was solid and square, with nothing that could be accused of being flashy; in fact, if you stand back and look at the side where the portico decorates the front door, it looks like a rich, safe bank. But when you move around and see the other two sides, you're impressed by the sheer scale of the place. Those windows are big and plentiful. (Remember, there was a tax on windows in those days.) The house is made of creamy Bath stone, and on a fine day it seems to soak up the sun.

The curious thing about Harford was that, although he wanted a sober house, he also got carried away by the fashions of his time for quaint frills and fripperies. He got a hot London architect, John Nash, to design him an orangery, all curves and glass, in which to grow exotic plants, and a thatched dairy, which has been well described as a piece of romantic nonsense (although it did function as a dairy).

Harford's son died childless in 1866, so his nephew inherited the estate. Unluckily, he too couldn't produce a

17

son, and after he died in 1875 his widow lived at Blaise with her three unmarried daughters for the next 44 years. She died in 1919, aged 90. The daughters decided they'd had enough of the family pile and went off to enjoy the fleshpots of Bath instead. In 1926 Bristol Corporation bought the Estate: one of the smartest moves it ever made.

Blaise Hamlet

Nash's orangery and dairy are pretty fancy, but for chocolate-box quaint, you've got to see the tiny hamlet that Nash designed for Harford. It makes Castle Combe look like Milton Keynes.

Blaise Hamlet is about 200 yards from the House, down Hallen Road. Harford used it as a kind of gingerbread retirement home for his elderly servants and tenants.

Nash arranged nine cottages around a green, with a pump in the middle. Each cottage is roughly the same size, and each has a hefty brick chimney, but otherwise they all look different — very different. Think of any Hans Andersen illustration you've ever seen. Now multiply it by ten, and you've got Blaise Hamlet. All the same, Nash made sure each cottage had its own loo, oven and copper for laundry, and people have lived here happily for nearly 200 years, so far be it from me to joke about the place. How many tower blocks of council flats will still be standing, let alone admired, 200 years from now?

The Big Fight: Goram v. Vincent

Two local giants, Goram and Vincent, fell in love with Avona, a Wiltshire beauty. In those days, a colossal lake stretched from Ashton Gate to Bradford-on-Avon. Avona promised to marry the giant who first drained it. Vincent decided to hack an opening through Durdham Down, which then stretched all the way to Failand. Goram chose to dig a channel through the Henbury Hills, which were also unbroken. The work made Goram thirsty, he drank too much beer, and he fell asleep in Goram's Chair. Vincent kept digging hard. In two hours he reached Sea Mills, drained the lake and so won Avona, who gave her name to Vincent's Avon Gorge. Goram woke up, slightly hungover and very cheesed-off at losing, and had a tantrum during which he stamped his foot and made Goram's Footprint. He then went off and drowned himself in the Severn: his head and shoulders still stick out and are now called Flat Holm and Steep Holm. That's the legend. It dates back over 400 years. Moral: Behind every successful gorge stands a gorgeous woman.

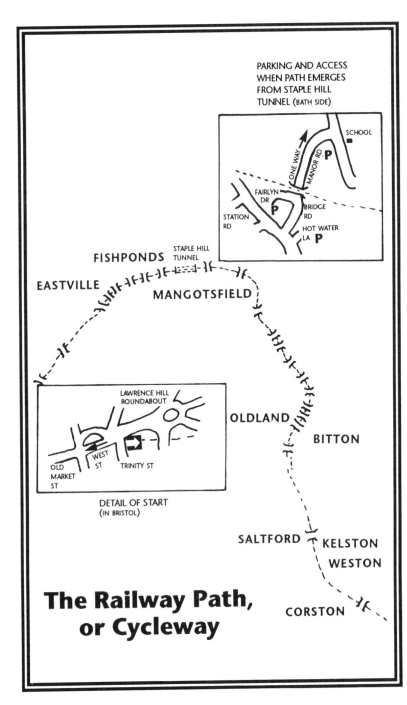

PARKING AND ACCESS
WHEN PATH EMERGES
FROM STAPLE HILL
TUNNEL (BATH SIDE)

SCHOOL

ONE WAY

MANOR RD

P

FAIRLYN
DR

P

STATION
RD

BRIDGE
RD

HOT WATER
LA P

FISHPONDS

STAPLE HILL
TUNNEL

EASTVILLE

MANGOTSFIELD

LAWRENCE HILL
ROUNDABOUT

OLDLAND

BITTON

OLD
MARKET
ST

WEST
ST

TRINITY ST

DETAIL OF START
(IN BRISTOL)

SALTFORD

KELSTON

WESTON

CORSTON

The Railway Path,
or Cycleway

THE RAILWAY PATH, OR CYCLEWAY

When visitors say what a lovely city Bristol is, they're usually not talking about Easton, Whitehall, Fishponds and all stops to Staple Hill. Let's face it: the eastern half of Bristol sprawls. The sad thing is that, in all this bricks-and-mortar, there are precious few good walks. That's why the Railway Path is such good news. It lets us walk, without fear of cars, trucks or motorbikes, from the heart of the city to the edge of the countryside — more than three miles — and then nearly all the way to Bath, another nine or ten miles of greenery. You can join it at dozens of points. Not surprisingly, the best bit is the green stretch. The rest is harmless and placid but a bit dull.

Railway Path: The City Stretch

This starts about halfway between Old Market Street and Lawrence Hill, where Trinity Street runs past a small city park. Trinity Street isn't exactly famous. Find West Street (a continuation of Old Market) and Trinity Street joins its end. But since West Street is one-way, a better approach might be by Clarence Road, which turns west out of the great Lawrence Hill roundabout and meets Trinity Street on the left.

21

Parking

Parking is easy near Trinity Street at weekends; at other times it's not. Try one of the residential streets near the major roads that cross the Railway Path nearby: Easton Road; Whitehall Road; Chelsea Road; Devon Road; Bruce Road; Johnsons Road. All these provide entry to the Path.

After that, it all depends where you want to join it. Get your road map out. There are access points at: Rose Green Road; Clay Bottom; Chapel Lane/Maggs Lane; Dominion Road; Parnall Road or Hockeys Lane (near Lodge Causeway); New Station Road/Filwood Road; Forest Road; Briar Way; Lower Station Road; and Acacia Avenue. After that you're into Staple Hill.

The Walk

Bristol slopes gently uphill to Staple Hill, and so does the Railway Path. It goes north-east past Lawrence Hill and Whitehall, and turns east at Fishponds to Staple Hill Tunnel, which pretty well marks the end of the city.

There's not an awful lot to be said about the City Stretch. It's lined with elder, bramble and buddleia, which is pleasant; however, it also shows you more of the bottoms of people's back gardens — rich in collapsed corrugated iron and black, mouldering heaps of lawn mowings — than you really want to see. It follows the old deep railway cuttings, which keep it quiet, but it often runs boringly straight.

There are few surprises. One is a great, gaunt factory; I discovered that they make Elizabeth Shaw chocolates here. I always had an image of the lovely Miss Shaw making her chocs one by one, in the wing of an elderly country rectory. Now I know better, and I wish I didn't.

Nearby, the landscape opens up to give a rare view of north Bristol, as far as Purdown with its Telecom Tower. In the foreground is Greenbank Cemetery. Look for the patches of uniform white headstones: war graves. Their dates tell their story. The earliest I found was 25 September 1940 — the day the Luftwaffe bombed Filton in daylight. Six bombs hit six shelters. Of 382 casualties, 100 died. Two are buried here. After that the dates are a calendar of the blitz. 24 November 1940 was a bad night. Ninety water mains were cut and Bristol burned like a beacon. 207 people were killed; ten lie in Greenbank, including the Rookes family, aged 41, 14 and 10. That tragedy was surpassed on 6 December 1940, when a bomb wiped out a family of seven. One simple headstone marks the grave of William and Carrie Isaacs (both 40), and Joyce, 15; Vera, 13; Willie, 12; Barbara, 10; and Norman, 8.

After Greenbank, the Railway Path offers the excitement of Clay Bottom Viaduct, but then it's a long mile of nothing much until Staple Hill Tunnel. Everyone should walk through a railway tunnel once in their life, and this is a juicy one.

For a start, it's long: over a quarter of a mile. When you go in, the light at the other end is the size of a penny. The tunnel is big and well lit, and it has a lovely sulphury smell, like a thousand coal fires on a foggy Saturday afternoon, the sort of smell that has become just a bronchial memory. I'd walked quite a long way into the tunnel before I realised that what I thought was a smoke-blackened lining is in fact a thick skin of soot, built up by the chuffing of decades of steam locomotives. Where the soot has peeled away, you can see a few of the millions of tiny bricks used to build the tunnel. The place has a gratifying echo: kids on bikes can't resist shouting as they belt into it.

Railway Path: The Green Stretch

A couple of hundred yards on the Bath side of Staple Hill

Tunnel, the Railway Path enters open fields, and from here on it's greenery all the way. What's more, high embankments improve the views.

Parking

What looks like the obvious place to join the Railway Path turns out to be a difficult spot for parking. It's where Bridge Road, which is a turning off Station Road, arrives from the south and becomes Manor Road going north. The Path crosses on a high bridge above the point where these two roads meet. If you're walking, you can't mistake the bridge because it's got I LOVE PIG painted on its north face in very faded white. Nearby is a large and eternally empty white noticeboard headed MANGOTSFIELD RURAL PARISH COUNCIL. The tracks next to this lead up to the Railway Path. Don't try to find a way to the Path on the south side of the bridge — Kraft Foods occupy all that land.

You won't see the I LOVE PIG sign if you're driving, because Manor Road is one-way going north (so you can't drive down it from Rodway Hill). This means that if you want to drive to the bridge you must come up Bridge Road. Parking here is not advisable, but what you can do is turn left off Bridge Road into Fairlyn Drive, about 25 yards from the bridge. This leads into a residential area where parking is easy. Then take the footpath under the bridge and climb the slope.

Manor Road is a winding, busy road; don't even think of parking on it. Instead, drive to the top and turn right (east) into Rodway Hill. Mangotsfield School is on your left and opposite it there is often good parking on the edge of the common. From here you can walk down and join the Railway Path, either near the bridge or — if you bear off to the left — near the ruined remains of Mangotsfield Station. When you reach a high, sheer cutting overlooking the station, continue left and a steep track takes you to a gateway.

If the parking spaces opposite the school are full, you won't find anything by driving on — Rodway Hill is nothing but dips and bends. Instead, try Elmsleigh Road, a side street to the left of the school.

On the other hand, if you prefer to join the Path a mile or so further east, follow Rodway Hill (which becomes Carsons Road) for just under a mile, to a T-junction. Turn right here (signposted to Warmley) and almost immediately fork left. Drive across Siston Common for one-third of a mile and you'll see Siston Bridge, which carries the Railway Path over the road. Don't drive under the bridge — instead, look for a space to park on your right or around the edge of the common.

There is an alternative. Take Station Road (the A4176, which runs from Mangotsfield to Warmley), go past Bridge Road and turn left into Hot Water Lane. (Honestly.) Park here. The lane becomes a track across a corner of Siston Common. Take the left fork, which eventually leads to a little tunnel, beyond which is a stile beside the Railway Path.

Railway Path: The Green Stretch: What You'll See

The surface is smooth and firm, suitable for prams, bikes or grans. The Path slopes gently downhill towards Bath, and it develops a series of gentle S-bends — very attractive: you keep walking to see what's around the corner.

The first landmark is the old Mangotsfield Station, about half a mile from the tunnel. It's on a big triangular site because this was a junction with a line that came down from the north. (It was, after all, the Midland Railway.) Much of the platform and the station building survive intact, and they give you an idea of how busy this line was in its heyday. Incidentally, that huge redbrick factory in the background is DRG Packaging.

A couple of hundred yards further on is where Avon County Council plans to obliterate this bit of Railway Path with a Ring Road, and replace it with a series of horrible right-angled detours to steer you back onto the Path again. Who knows? Maybe Avon itself will vanish in a puff of blue smoke first.

Then the Path crosses Siston Common. By now you're well into the country, so it comes as a surprise to find yourself not only in Warmley but actually having to cross a major road, the A420. It won't happen again. From here on, the Path curves south to Oldland, a lot of it in a cutting. Bitton Station, a good two miles from Mangotsfield Station, is where the Avon Valley Railway runs its steam trains over a short length of track next to the Path; the refreshment room operates at weekends.

Now the countryside really opens up, and beyond Bitton you get splendid views of the southern Cotswolds on one side and the wandering Avon on the other. If you've gone this far, you're nearer Bath than Bristol, and all that remains for me to say is goodbye and good luck.

Access points after Warmley are many, and usually near bridges. Look for: St Ivel Way; Tweeny Lane (near Poplar Road); Southway Drive (near Victoria Road); Millers Drive; North Street; West Street; Meadow Court Drive; School Road (off Barry Road); Cherry Garden Lane; and finally Bitton Station. After that, look for access points wherever the Path crosses the Avon, especially at Saltford.

THE FROME VALLEY WALK

You've almost certainly seen the River Frome, even if you didn't recognise it. Driving out of Bristol on the M32, just before Eastville Stadium you look down on a stream walled in by concrete. It's the Frome. If you park near the Eastville roundabout under the M32, you can walk for the best part of three miles alongside the Frome, through a wonderful variety of countryside, from watermeadows to minor gorges to timbered valleys. On either side there may be houses only a hundred yards away — yet they are usually shut out from sight or sound. What's more, most of the first stretch in Bristol is easy, level going, even for prams or grans, and you won't need big boots. (After that it gets muddy.) The Frome Valley is a great, green place to go for a stroll at any time of year.

Parking

Parking is easy at several places up (or down, depending where you live) the Frome, so you can walk a short stretch of the river or do the lot, as you wish.

Starting at Eastville Park:
Parking Near the Lower Entrance

Take the Eastville Tesco as a landmark. From the great roundabout next to it, Stapleton Road runs north — look for a sign pointing to FRENCHAY B4058. Not much space for

27

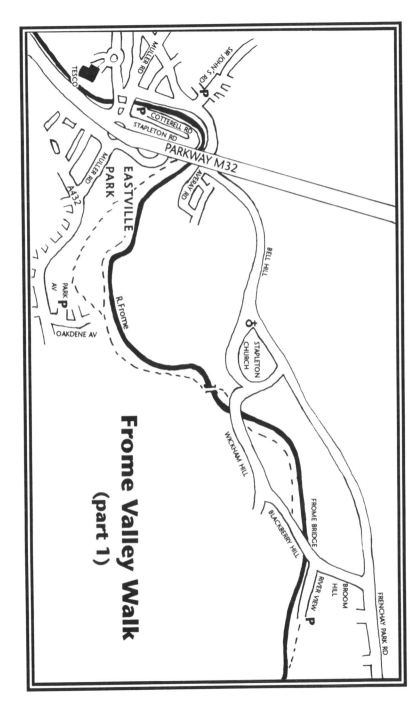

Frome Valley Walk
(part 1)

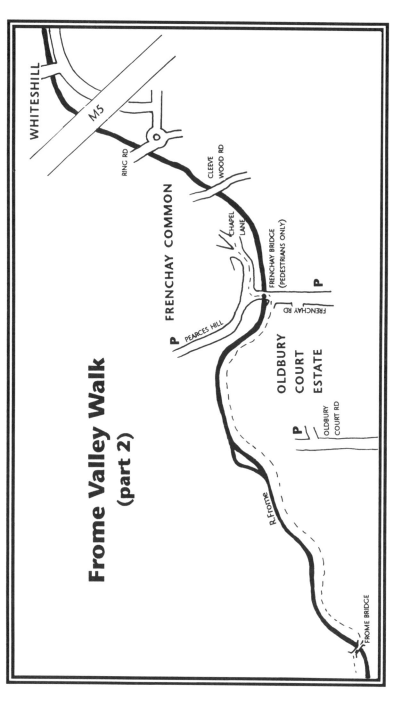

Frome Valley Walk (part 2)

WHITESHILL

M5

RING RD

CLEEVE WOOD RD

FRENCHAY COMMON

CHAPEL LANE

FRENCHAY BRIDGE (PEDESTRIANS ONLY)

P

P

PEARCES HILL

FRENCHAY RD

OLDBURY COURT ESTATE

P

OLDBURY COURT RD

R.Frome

FROME BRIDGE

parking on Stapleton Road, but it's worth trying the first left turn, Cottrell Road, a dead end. The second left turn, Glenfrome Road, isn't a good bet (too busy) but it has a side street, Sir John's Lane, which is promising. Alternatively, turn right from Stapleton Road into Averay Road, a long dead-end with side streets — lots of space here. Some people park under the M32 itself.

Starting at Eastville Park:
Parking Near the Top Entrance

At the big Eastville roundabout, take Muller Road eastward, alongside the park. At the first traffic lights you merge with Fishponds Road. Follow this through another set of lights. Watch for an off-licence, then turn left into Oakdene Avenue; then left again into Park Avenue. At its end is a surprisingly big (30-40 spaces) car-park right on the edge of Eastville Park.

Parking Near Frome Bridge

Frome Bridge is about a mile up the Frome from the Eastville roundabout.

Stapleton Road becomes Bell Hill which becomes Park Road. After a Jet station, at a mini-roundabout, turn right into Broom Hill, which leads down to Frome Bridge. (If you're approaching from the south, turn off Fishponds Road at Manor Road; this leads to Blackberry Hill which eventually meets Broom Hill at Frome Bridge.) Bang next to the bridge and parallel with the river is River View. It usually looks hopeless for parking: a narrow dead-end stiff with cars. Do not be put off. Drive in, because at the other end is quite a big car-park (50-60 spaces).

If, however, this is full, go back to the mini-roundabout on Park Road and turn right. Take the second turning right,

Sheldrake Drive, which leads right into a network of side streets where parking is easy. Now you have to walk back to River View, I'm afraid.

Parking Near Frenchay Road Bridge

About a mile above Frome Bridge, Frenchay Road arrives from the south and makes a bridge to join Frenchay Hill on the north. Be warned; concrete bollards prevent cars from crossing this bridge. Frenchay Hill is very cramped for parking. Better to park in Frenchay Road. There's room for four or five cars beside the bridge and plenty of space further back, on Frenchay Road or in its side streets.

  If you must park on the Frenchay side of the bridge, you'll be very lucky to find a space on Pearces Hill or Frenchay Hill. However, Frenchay Common is nearby (at the top of Pearces Hill) and it offers plenty of room. Opposite the White Lion, a stretch of roadside car-park has 15 spaces. If all else fails, try Church Road, just around the corner from the pub.

Parking at Oldbury Court Estate

Midway between Frome Bridge and Frenchay Road Bridge, on the south side of the Frome, is Oldbury Court Estate, which runs down to the river itself. So you can drive here, park, walk through the Estate (which is a public park) and join the Frome pathway. To get there, follow Oldbury Court Road (a turning off Fishponds Road) to the end, where there is a big car-park (100 spaces).

Short Walk: Eastville Park to Frome Bridge

It's easy to find the Frome once you get into Eastville Park: just keep going downhill. On your way you might stroll around the lake, which is full of exotic ducks and suchlike. The swans, sensible animals, prefer to live on the Frome, where they don't have to watch labradors endlessly retrieving bits of wood and looking tremendously pleased with themselves.

If you parked in the Park Avenue space, take a look, as you walk down the slope, at that curious three-sided brick building. Back in 1915 they built an open-air pool there. Millions of people happily splashed about in it until November 1940, when the Luftwaffe mistook it for a military target and bombed it. By a nice coincidence, this bit of park is now a Sri Chinmoy Peace Mile: a measured mile where runners can find inner peace, Sri Chinmoy being a meditator who enjoyed running.

The path beside the Frome is flat and level, and the surface is tarmac, so you can bring the pushchair or gran or both.

The River Frome meanders along amiably over this first section. That large church is Holy Trinity, put up in 1857 when Stapleton became a rich little suburb and felt like letting everybody know. Nearer is Colston's School, a very sporting establishment: note the rugby pitches. They can fish the rugby balls out of the Frome easily enough, but in summer lose a few cricket balls, which, alas, do not float. Look up: you might see squirrels, and even a hovering falcon.

The scenery matches the pace of the river: green and gentle, never spectacular but always changing. So this is a good moment to reflect on the part in history played by what looks today like an unimportant stream.

The Frome is one half of the reason why Bristol is where it is. The Avon twists and turns and makes its final bend into Bristol from the north-east. Just a short distance away, the Frome also comes in from the north-east. Originally (that is, before the Cut was dug), the Avon turned west and joined the Frome. This created a long thumb of rocky land between the two rivers, just before the join. On this rocky strip, at a point where the rivers came close, Bristol Castle was built — protected by water on two sides. Bristol's centre is very low-lying. Most of the old town is much less than 100 feet above sea level, which explains why the word 'marsh' appears so often on town maps: Canon's Marsh, St Philip's Marsh, Marsh Street. The ridge between Frome and Avon is only 50 feet above sea level, but that was enough. It made a good site for a bridge place, which in those days they called a Brig Stowe or Bricgstow, which in time got smoothed into Bristol. Even then, you see, they were adding a final 'L'.

Now back to the walk.

After half a mile or so you can see the beginnings of a little gorge where the Frome has carved a path through Pennant sandstone. Take the footbridge over the river and walk up a short meadow to a roadway. Turn right and it takes you to Wickham Bridge. There's been a bridge here for several centuries. Look ahead up the hill and red gables show on the skyline — the roof of Wickham Court, 300 years old.

Cross the bridge and turn left into a much longer, wider meadow. In summer, wild plants grow in great variety by the Frome, and very attractive they are. Never eat them. None will do you any good and some — hemlock, for instance — will poison you very thoroughly.

Watch the woodland that rises on the other side of the Frome and you won't see any badgers (they come out at night) but you might see where they've dug out red earth. Badgers are enthusiastic tunnellers. Many foxes live near the Frome; they too can excavate great amounts of earth.

The meadow ends at Frome Bridge. Climb the stile at the side of a row of cottages and turn right, up the steps to Blackberry Hill. If you want to keep going up the Frome Valley, cross the bridge and turn right into River View.

Short Walk: Frome Bridge to Frenchay Village

This is the most popular stretch of the Frome Valley Walk, because it has a sort of rugged grandeur in miniature — huge overhanging rocks and massive trees, plenty of throbbing weirs, lots of wilderness on either bank and ample bird life — and the Frome is constantly twisting, so you keep getting a fresh view.

The car-park at the end of River View used to be a quarry — Stapleton Church was built of Pennant stone taken from here — and the cottages themselves were lived in by quarrymen's families. After the Second World War, the quarry was filled with rubble from bombed bits of Bristol. (This is an honour it shares with the foundations of the East Side Highway in Manhattan; freighters sailing from Avonmouth to New York to collect war supplies used to carry bricks and stone from blitzed buildings as ballast.) The car-park has two amenities: public toilets at the far end, and The Chalet at the near end. The Chalet is where Mrs Marjorie Pickett sells snacks and drinks and such like. What's more, she's been doing it since 1948, which is a lot of cups of tea. She opens The Chalet every day of the year except Christmas Day and Boxing Day. Stop and say hello and buy something. Marj is a great local institution.

The walk begins at the far end of the car-park. First you come to the remains of the old snuff mills (probably really an old corn mill), with flower gardens alongside — a good spot for a picnic. Plenty of songbirds around here, thanks to plantations of spruce and larch. You might hear the old favourites (blackbird, wren, robin, willow warbler) as well as wood pigeons, collared doves, magpies and chiffchaffs.

Then the path winds alongside the river for a mile, nearly all of it metalled, and it enters what's really a small-scale gorge. The rock strata run horizontally, and as the rush of the Frome and the battering of the climate have worn them away, they have created unusual shoulders of stone. Above and below these projections grow hulking great oaks and beeches. Happily, the effect of the natural death and decay of the woods has not been tidied up. Where trees have fallen, they are left to lie, even if they crashed into the river. This is a walk where you spend half your time looking up. Naturally, it's a wonderful area for birds. Keep an eye out for kingfishers.

Weirs trap the Frome every hundred yards, it seems. This was a thriving business park, centuries ago. Each weir fed water to a mill — originally corn mills, although later some became snuff or flock mills. There was even a brass wire mill down at Baptist Mills, below Eastville, 300 years ago.

A few hundred yards above Frome Bridge, a small stream comes in from the right (assuming you're walking upstream). Follow this and it leads up into Oldbury Court Estate. If you want to stretch your walk you could stroll around here. It's a pleasant, spacious place with shrub and flower gardens, an arboretum, a children's playground (thoroughly fenced-in) and public toilets near the playground. It's big enough to allow for horseriding, football and cricket pitches, plus a nicely secluded rugby pitch where I have refereed many a game, always to the general approval of not only the teams but also the spectator, although his dog sometimes fell asleep. Having said all that, I should add that Oldbury Court Estate is definitely a neat and tidy park, almost manicured, as compared with the rough-and-ready Frome Valley. This whole area was part of Kingswood Chase in medieval times. There was a hunting lodge here, and then Oldbury Court was built on the site; but nothing's left of either.

You can return to the Frome path the way you came, or you can work your way across Oldbury Court in a north-easterly direction, over another stream and past the rugby pitch, to a track that leads down through the woods to the Frome. (By doing so you will have missed a lot of good river scenery, but never mind: you can see it on your way back.)

Before long, the waterside path ceases to have its solid metalled surface, and the last couple of hundred yards before Frenchay Bridge are definitely not for prams or grans. The path snakes and switchbacks above the river, and there is no fence, so keep a firm grip on your offspring, or you might find yourself fishing them out of the drink.

At Frenchay Bridge (bollarded to stop cars crossing) the longterm path crosses to the other side of the Frome. You can, if you wish, walk straight on without crossing the bridge. The path becomes narrow, slippery and broken, but it persists for a few hundred yards, before it runs into a wire fence. There's a hole, which you can explore, but you won't get far. Someone has painted on a beech tree, in tiny white, flaking letters: I LOVE FAY FROM NICK. I hope his love lasts longer than his paint.

FVW - the Frome Valley Walkway
Out of Frenchay

Cross Frenchay Road Bridge and turn right into the village. A few yards up the hill, turn right into Chapel Lane, signposted for the Frome Valley Walkway — abbreviated from now on to FVW. The FVW path follows a riverside field (often muddy), or you can walk the hillside above it — this is Frenchay Moor and it's National Trust. All too soon it ends when Cleve Road crosses the Frome.

Here, a FVW sign shows you where you've come from; pity it doesn't also tell you where to go next. Cross the road and enjoy the view upstream. The Mill House (now a private residence) is well worth a glance. But don't turn right. You'll be wasting your time looking for a public path on that side of the Frome. Turn left (away from the bridge) and follow the road uphill for about 150 yards. Turn right into Grange Park. On the left, between house numbers 8 and 9, a metal plate set in the ground points down an alley to the FVW.

From this point onwards, the Frome is less tamed and disciplined — no more weirs, for instance, and occasionally the water bubbles over rocks, with even a small waterfall or two. On either side you pass rugged stands of overhanging rock that are typical of this valley. In fact the next half mile of the FVW is a delightful walk, well shielded from housing, rich in hefty trees and wildlife — squirrels, wild duck, many varieties of other birds. I saw a kingfisher here: metallic blue, streaking downstream.

The path is fairly flat and level, gravelled to start with but muddy in patches thereafter. One thing you can't escape is the noise of traffic, because the FVW passes under the Avon Ring Road and the M4. The racket's pretty awful, but the lofty pillars of the Ring Road Bridge are handsome in their way. Concrete stairs lead down to the FVW from the Ring Road. You can reach them by walking along the pavement from the huge Bromley Heath roundabout to the east, or from the Frenchay crossroads to the west.

A hundred yards beyond the M4 bridge, a pretty little footbridge marks the point where the FVW forks left up a lane. Take a breather here. Lean on the bridge and look at the red-and-white poles hanging above the water: almost certainly canoe slalom poles. Gives you an idea how high the Frome can rise when the rains come. This is partly because Bradley Brook joins the Frome about 50 yards upstream. Look for the FVW signpost here, on the right. A few yards away is the White Horse pub and the Roadhouse Diner, at Whiteshill — not a bad spot to park if you prefer to start here and walk down the Frome.

From here on, the FVW — partly on roads, partly on green

paths — heads north through farmland for Winterbourne, Frampton Cotterell, and its source as a mere trickle in Dodington Park on the Cotswold edge.

(For more information on birds, trees and plants, see the excellent *Frome Valley Visitors Guide & Nature Trail*. You might be able to buy a copy at The Chalet.)

THE TOWPATH THROUGH THE AVON GORGE

This is the longest green walk in Bristol: four miles from its start at the Cumberland Basin to its end at Pill. Since it goes through the Avon Gorge, it's also highly spectacular, and being a towpath it's easy to walk. The surface for the first mile or so is good enough for grans and bikes, so it might even be good enough for pushchairs too, depending on the weather. The rest of the path can get a bit muddy. Don't wear daps in the monsoon season.

Parking

At the foot of Rownham Hill, a short lane leads to the towpath, but at the time of writing it's crammed with travellers' vehicles. No hope of parking there. That leaves the Cumberland Basin area. There are two possible sites: one on the Hotwells side, the other on the opposite side.

Parking on the Hotwells Side

Let's assume you're driving along Hotwell Road (either from the Portway or from the City) and you turn into Merchants Road (which leads traffic towards the Plimsoll Bridge and the Cumberland Basin Flyover). Merchants Road widens and forms three lanes. Take the centre lane, signposted A4 to Avonmouth. This swings right and runs

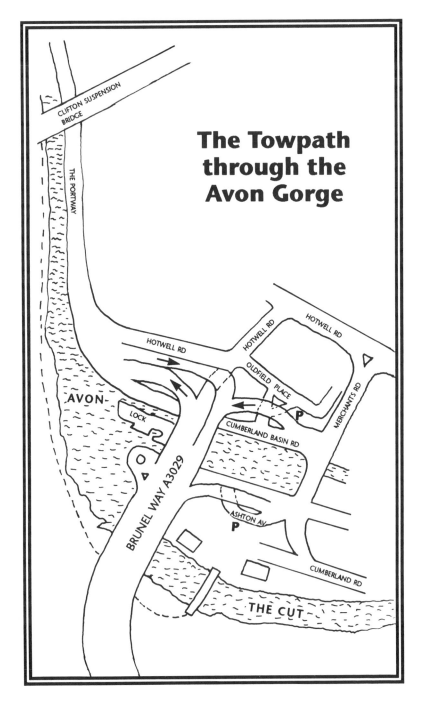

The Towpath through the Avon Gorge

CLIFTON SUSPENSION BRIDGE

THE PORTWAY

HOTWELL RD

HOTWELL RD

HOTWELL RD

HOTWELL RD

OLDFIELD PLACE

MERCHANTS RD

AVON

LOCK

P

CUMBERLAND BASIN RD

BRUNEL WAY A3029

ASHTON AV

P

CUMBERLAND RD

THE CUT

alongside the docks. Almost immediately, look for signs painted on the right of the road surface saying CITY CITY CITY and leading into a turn-off to the right, called Faraday Road. At once another right turn appears, with 'P' parking signs. This quickly leads to Oldfield Place. On your right is a car-park with about 20 spaces. If this is full, try Oldfield Place (a cul-de-sac) or the streets turning off it. There is a sign pointing to SUBWAY & TOILETS, but the toilets must be well hidden. I couldn't find them.

Parking on the Opposite Side

This time, when you turn into Merchants Road, take the left-hand lane and go straight on over the narrow bridge, following signs that say 'Transport Café'. At the end of the bridge, just beyond the Nova Scotia pub, the road forks. Take the right fork and immediately turn left into Ashton Avenue, a short redbrick terrace — still following the promise of a transport café. If you can't park here, go 50 yards on and there's usually space under the highway, next to the transport cafe, which has been defunct for as long as I can remember. While you're getting out of the car, look across at the great curving terraces of Regency Clifton — seen at their best from this viewpoint. Note: Beware traffic wardens in Ashton Avenue! They have appeared after nearly 20 tranquil years and begun bothering motorists.

Getting to the Towpath From Hotwells

You have a choice of two routes — across the docks, or over the Plimsoll Bridge.

In either case, start walking under the highway, through a forest of concrete pillars, and cross the A4. On the right of the bridge, next to a spiral staircase, is a gateway onto the dockside. Be warned: it's a long fall into that deep water, so if you have volatile or uncontrollable children in your charge, now is the time to keep them away from the edge and take them up the spiral stairs instead. If, on the other hand, your party is totally sane and well-balanced, you can cross the lock by that narrow footbridge with white chains as handrails. Another warning: there is no public right of way in the docks. You're not prohibited entry, but watch your step.

You're now in the central section of the docks. On the far side, where the Avon flows nearby, you can see a colossal wooden rack down on the mud. Ships park themselves here, so that running repairs can be made at low tide, while the ship is lashed to the dockside to keep it upright. Before the Floating Harbour provided permanently wet moorings in Bristol, sailing ships fell over sideways every time the tide went out. Given Bristol's steep mudbanks and great rise and fall of tide, they fell hard. Ships built here had to be extra-strong, or as the shipbuilders said, built 'Bristol-fashion'. Now you know.

Next, walk over the steel bridge (on the right of the Plimsoll Bridge) and cross the road and go left under the Plimsoll Bridge. There are public toilets here.

A vast nine-storey redbrick warehouse faces you. Go round its left-hand side. (The right-hand side is sometimes locked.) Ahead you see the old railway bridge over the Avon. It carries a tarmac path. On the other side, turn right, follow the path under the Flyover, and aim for the Gorge. The towpath soon appears beside the railway.

That's the interesting (if slightly longwinded) route. The alternative is simple. Go up the spiral staircase, walk over the Plimsoll Bridge and go down the next spiral staircase. Then walk up the right-hand pavement to the Flyover. After a hundred yards there's an exit into the park. It's a noisy route, but if you plan it right you won't have to cross the traffic.

Getting to the Towpath From the Opposite Side

If you parked in or near Ashton Avenue, walk up the dockside road, under the Plimsoll Bridge, and follow the right-hand pavement onto the Flyover, which leads to an exit into the park, where the path to the Gorge is pretty obvious. Or you can go past the redbrick warehouse, cross the Avon by the old railway bridge, then turn right and follow the path towards the Gorge.

The Towpath Walk

This walk couldn't be more simple. There's only one path, and it runs close to the river, that being the best way to tow ships. The Avon is a tricky enough piece of water for powered ships to navigate, so you can imagine the problems it posed for sailing ships. Each arrival had to stop at Pill and collect its tow — usually horse, sometimes rowing boats.

There's plenty to look at here. Half the history of Bristol is visible from the start of this walk.

Look back at the Cumberland Basin: that lockgate is where the old Avon used to emerge. Now look back at the river itself. That channel is known as 'The Cut', because it was hacked out by navvies and French prisoners-of-war nearly 200 years ago, so that the river would by-pass the Floating Harbour. The Cut goes as far as Totterdown: two miles that took five years to dig.

Look up at Clifton, at those rich town houses poised high above Hotwells, once a spa. There is an actual well, not so much hot as tepid, and for a while the smart set came here to drink the stuff, which tastes disgusting and has no medicinal value. That was when Bristol began to count as something more than a big seaport, and Brunel brought his Great Western Railway here. The city fathers chose Brunel's plan for Clifton Suspension Bridge. (He had another design that showed the roadway emerging from tunnels high in the Gorge, but that was too exciting for them.) Ask yourself: why build a bridge up there? It didn't link Clifton with anything special on the other side, 150 years ago. No, our Victorian forebears did it out of pure swank. They had the wealth, Brunel had the know-how, and if you've got it, flaunt it. Incidentally, the whole thing weighs 2,400 tons and the chains were secondhand when they bought them.

Near the Suspension Bridge, the Gorge rears up at its most sheer and most impressive. This is a mighty split in the landscape, and it wasn't made by the Avon. Rivers have terrific power to erode, but in this case the Gorge came first and the Avon followed. (Just think for a moment: why should the Avon try to batter its way through 300 feet of solid rock when there is an easier route to the Severn, between the Dundry Hills and the Failand Hills? If the river preceded the Gorge, it would have done what the railway did, and gone to Weston via Long Ashton, Nailsea and Yatton.)

The rock is strong, which is why the walls of the Gorge are so vertical, and why climbers like it. On a good day you can see pairs of them dotted all over the face, linked by bright ropes. By rock-climbing standards, the Gorge has sections that are easy, medium-tough, grim and terrifying. The terrifying bits occur where the climber has to climb outwards in order to get over a protruding lump. This is not especially difficult unless you think it is, when it becomes a nightmare. Personally, I'll stick to squash and backgammon. Incidentally, some faces of the Gorge are old quarries, where the rock is unreliable, which explains the absence of climbers. There are many more old quarries on the towpath side, and a right mess they made of the landscape, too.

The Gorge reaches its geological climax at the cliffs of Durdham Down known as the Sea Walls. After that it widens and falls away into Old Sneed Park (a suburb which exists, like the cavalry in war, to lend a certain tone to what would otherwise be a vulgar brawl). The towpath side ceases to be overhung by the Forestry Commission and goes past wide fields.

This is where the Avon, having made a feint to the north, swerves north-west at Sea Mills harbour, and then collides with Shirehampton Park and turns sharp south-west. The result is the notorious Horseshoe Bend. It put the hex on Bristol docks because the bend is so tight that any ship more than about 330 feet long can't get through it. 330 feet is still quite useful, and during World War Two I often watched, from the vantage-point of the playground of St Edyth's Mixed Infants School, as a steady traffic of freighters and warships passed Sea Mills. With the peace, ships got longer but the Horseshoe Bend stayed the same, and eventually the traffic went elsewhere.

As the Avon leaves the Bend and starts to curve westerly for the Severn, the towpath ends half a mile short of Pill, where a little inlet forces you to turn inland and skirt a field. Leave by a stile and follow the lane for a few hundred yards into the grounds of Ham Green Hospital, where — if you're lucky — someone will be waiting with a car. If not, it's four miles back to the Cumberland Basin. The Gorge looks even better going back.

Starting From Pill

If you live in Shirehampton, Avonmouth, Portishead or Clevedon, you might prefer to walk the towpath from Pill to Bristol. Find Ham Green Hospital (amply signposted) and drive in until you reach the final roundabout. A smallish (20 space) car-park is to your right, and I see no reason why you shouldn't use it, since the hospital itself has virtually closed down. Dead ahead a sign says: 'PRIVATE ROAD. No unauthorised access.' Do not be discouraged. This is a 'Cyclebag' route, officially okay for cyclists to take the towpath to Bristol, so walkers should press on. Follow the lane, past a long and pretty lake on your right and some terraced houses on your left, until you see a handsome white farmhouse ahead. The stile is to its right. Keep to the edge of the field.

PRIOR'S WOOD, PORTBURY

Not to be confused with the Royal Portbury Dock on the north side of the M5. This Portbury is the original tiny village, just south of the M5. Prior's Wood is small — not much more than half a mile long — but it's off on its own, very quiet, and perfect for a short stroll.

Parking

If you're crossing the Avonmouth Bridge (M5) heading south, take the first exit (19), marked Gordano Services. Ignore the Services and take the next turn-off to the left, marked A369 to Easton-in-Gordano and Clifton. After 50 yards turn right (signposted Portbury).

If you're driving out from Bristol on the A369 (Portishead) road, take this same turning on your left, just as the M5 comes in sight.

Okay. Follow this turning for about half a mile and you enter the village of Portbury. At this point the main road turns sharp left but you keep going straight ahead on the High Street (signposted PORTBURY CLAPTON NAILSEA). Then take the next left turn (signposted CLAPTON & NAILSEA — also GORDANO RFC) into Caswell Lane. Ahead you'll see a mock-Tudor gatehouse with green timbering and a steep tiled roof. Beside it is a metal farm gate, with a pedestrian gate to its right. There's also a sign saying 'Private, No Horses , No Vehicles, Please Keep Dogs On Lead.' The walk starts here. Park in Caswell Lane.

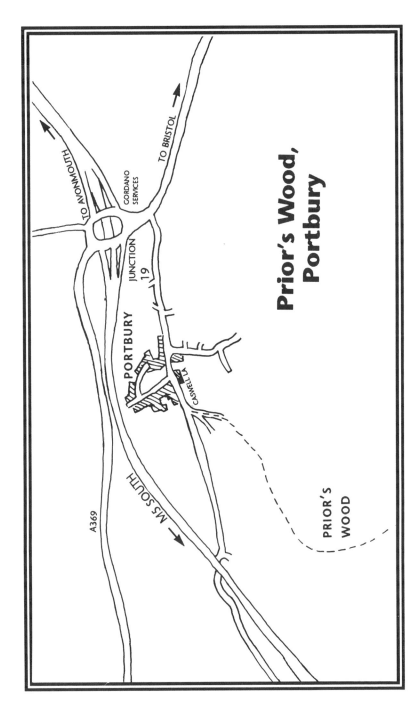

The Walk in Prior's Wood

The first stretch is a simple climb, not steep but stony and no place for pushchairs, although most grans should be able to cope. Quite soon, the mighty roar of the M5 fades and, amazingly, the tranquillity of the woods takes over completely. Then, at the top of the hill, you reach a scene of silent carnage. Early in 1990 a storm came blasting out of the Atlantic, was funnelled by the Severn, and hit the middle of Prior's Wood like a bomb. A dozen enormous beeches — their roots already weakened by a previous gale — crashed in the space of minutes. Some still lie here.

The path emerges from the trees, becomes a tarmac drive and crosses some fine, rolling farmland with good views all around, before it enters more woodland. The Downs School is on the left. The final quarter of a mile to the B3128 was completely blocked with fallen trees during the Great Gale, but plenty of handsome specimens are still standing. And that's that, really. Turn round and walk back. An enjoyable hour or so, at any time of year.

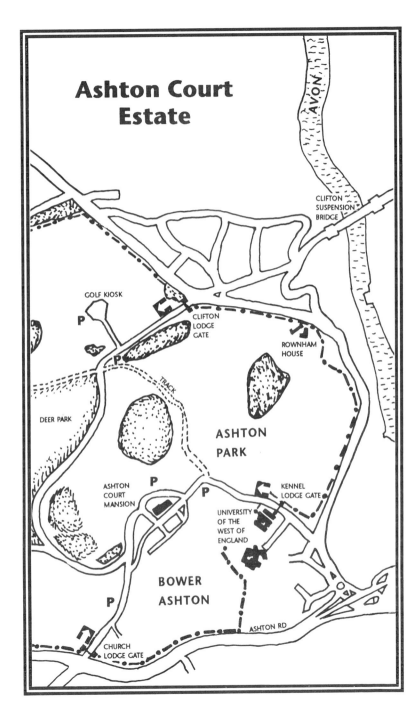

ASHTON COURT ESTATE

Every Bristolian thinks they know all about Ashton Court, if only because the hot air balloon fiesta is held there. But I bet nine out of ten Bristolians have never explored three-quarters of the Estate. Most visitors look at the mansion, walk around the nearest wood, and then settle down with their sandwiches while the kids argue about whether that was a goal, stupid.

And why not? Ashton Court is a good place for a short walk. It sprawls all over the hillside, and there are huge grassy spaces, so you always know where you are. The views over south Bristol and across to Dundry are fine. But a touch of curiosity pays great dividends, because then you discover that Ashton Court goes on and on to the west. It covers 850 acres in all. You can walk through large, unspoiled plantations. The biggest stretch of woodland is well over a mile long. You can spend half the day exploring this place without ever re-crossing your path.

Parking

In 1810 Sir Hugh Smyth enclosed Ashton Court Estate with a high wall, most of which still stands. The only way in or out is via the various lodges, and not all of them are open to the public. In fact there are only three places where you can drive in: Clifton Lodge Gate at the top; Church Lodge Gate at the bottom; and Kennel Lodge Gate on the right hand side.

Clifton Lodge Gate

This is half a mile from the Suspension Bridge, at the top of Rownham Hill, on the A369. Drive in here. No parking beside the road: a string of logs prevents it. After a quarter of a mile, a right turn vanishes over the hill. It looks less than promising, but in fact it leads to a big gravelled car-park (75 spaces) at the pitch-and-putt kiosk and fast-food outlet. Public toilets here. Alternatively, drive on and turn left after 50 yards to a dirt car-park (40 or 50 spaces, according to the intelligence of the drivers). A gate on the road may stop you going any further — it's sometimes impossible to drive right through the Estate (for instance, at weekends and holidays).

Kennel Lodge Gate

Coming from central Bristol, take the A369 (Portishead) road at the end of the Cumberland Basin system. The road ducks under the Flyover, crosses a roundabout and is then called Clanage Road. After 200 yards, turn left into Kennel Lodge Road, signposted to Ashton Court Mansion.

(To reach this point from the opposite direction, drive past Clifton Lodge Gate, down Rownham Hill into Clanage Road, then turn sharp right into Kennel Lodge Road.)

Kennel Lodge is a modest, grey-stone cottage; you'll pass it without noticing. The gate (which is shut at dusk) is beyond Bower Ashton College of Art. Just inside the Estate there's a very bumpy bit of parking (12 spaces). The road then bends behind the Mansion, where there is space for 20-30 cars.

Church Lodge Gate

From the Cumberland Basin system, take the A370 (the Weston Road) but stay in the left lane and make a rapid exit onto the B3128. You won't need much of this, either. After a few hundred yards there is a left fork to Long Ashton. Directly opposite, on your right, is Church Lodge Gate. The Lodge entrance is narrow and oncoming traffic can be a bit brisk, not to mention the stuff coming out of Long Ashton, so mind how you go, squire. Drive up the slope into the Estate and you'll find half a dozen parking places at the roadside. Or you can drive on and park behind the Mansion, as already described.

Over the Wall

I said there are only three ways to drive in, and so there are; but if they all turn out to be hopeless, you can always try parking in North Road, which is a turning off the A369 near the Beggars Bush Lane traffic lights, or in one of the side roads off North Road.

Then walk across the A369. Near the bus stop is an iron gate. It's always locked but the wall is so low you can climb over it.

Public Toilets

As well as those on the top of the Estate at the golf kiosk, there are public toilets in the old stable block courtyard, which is at the east (or Bristol) end of the Mansion.

High Days, Balloon Fiestas and Agricultural Shows

All the above advice about parking goes right out of the window when the sun shines on special occasions. Parts of Ashton Court may then be opened especially for parking. (You may have to pay.) All the same, there are days when the mob is so dense that you're probably better off parking in Clifton and walking over the bridge. For one thing, you'll save the parking fee, and for another, you'll avoid the endless queuing to get out, which has destroyed more marriages than gin.

The Visitor Centre

This is in the old stable block which forms the east wing of the Mansion. It's open at weekends, or by special arrangement (phone 0117 9639174). Any school planning a visit should certainly contact the Visitor Centre first. It's run by Naomi Wright and Bernice Keith, and — as I discovered — they are enormously helpful.

Ashton Court Mansion: An Instant History

The manor of Long Ashton is listed in the Domesday Book, so it must have been there in 1066. By 1280 a manor house existed on the site of the present Mansion. In 1392, Richard II permitted Thomas de Lyons to enclose the land and make a deer park — in those days deer-hunting was a royal privilege. Herds of red and fallow deer wandered freely over the Estate for the next 547 years; that is, until World War Two. Meanwhile, after various changes of ownership, a Bristol merchant called John Smyth bought the Estate in 1545.

The Smyths lived here for 400 years, extended the Mansion, planted vast numbers of trees, and made a packet out of the coal mines in Ashton Vale. The coal ran out in 1914 and the family expired in 1946, when the last in the line, Esme Smyth, died. By now the family fortune was spent. The deer escaped, the roof began to fall in, the place went to the dogs. Bristol Corporation got the Estate in 1959, knocked down several buildings before they collapsed, and began restoration work in 1974. Today the Mansion looks good. You can book it for your wedding reception, if you like.

Short Walk: The Prairie

If you park by the pitch-and-putt kiosk, you're on a high, wide, sweeping plateau. If you like prairie, and if the wind isn't too blustery, turn your back on Bristol and keep walking until you've seen enough grass. Then turn downhill, cross a stony path and plunge into the nearest wood. When you've seen enough trees, turn left and any path will bring you out. Climb through the golfers and eventually you'll see your car.

Short Walk: From Kennel Lodge Gate

Instead of forking left towards the Mansion, head on uphill, keeping to the right of a big mixed wood (Summerhouse Plantation). Somewhere here is the largest tree in Bristol: an oak whose trunk measures 40 feet around. Climb the stile and keep climbing. Turn right after the gate and go up the lane to the golf course. Take a breather and enjoy the view, including the lime avenue, planted by the Smyths to point towards the Suspension Bridge. Now walk down the other side of the Summerhouse Plantation, and pay your respects to the so-called Domesday Oak, which is certainly not 900-plus years old but still needs crutches to prop it up. Carry on around the Mansion and you're back where you started.

Short Walk: Around the Deer Park

If you came in through Church Lodge Gate, the Deer Park is easy to see, on your left. If you came from other directions, you find it by following the road down to, or up from, the Mansion, which runs alongside it. Now turn your back on the Mansion and walk along the path beside the bottom fence of the Deer Park, and you find yourself in Clarken Coombe Wood. Fork right after 200 yards, do the same again at the next junction, and this path will lead you to the open hillside above the topmost corner of the Deer Park, after which it's downhill all the way.

Long Walks

It all depends where you start from; in any case, most of Ashton Court is so wide open that you can do your own navigation without my advice. But for what it's worth, here's a long walk that shows you the best of the Estate, yet takes you away from the thronging crowds.

Start at the golf kiosk car-park and walk away from Bristol. The turf is bouncy, obstacles are none, you can step it out. A stony track rises from your left, heading in much the same way. After a good half mile, this track starts to run alongside the edge of New Barn Wood, on your left. Take any of several wandering paths through this shaggy bit of woodland, and at the other end you'll meet a track going gently downhill, beside a big meadow. It leads into the depths of Clarken Coombe Wood and connects there with the main path. Turn right and you have more than half a mile of unbroken woodland ahead of you before you hit the boundary wall.

Turn back and, as the fancy seizes you, explore some of the side-paths that fall away to your right. Everything links up and eventually leads you more or less towards the Mansion, but this is such a marvellously varied little forest, full of twists and turns, gullies and dips and rises, that it's a shame to hurry. And the trees are worth seeing. Some of the stoutest, if not the tallest, oaks grow in groups; they must have been here since Tudor times, at least. There are also small redwoods — small meaning taller than anything else

— and whole hillsides covered with youngish beeches. Much of this was planted by the Smyths, not just to make timber but to look good; and today we get the benefit of their foresight.

This mile-long stretch of woods comes to an end high above the Mansion. Walk down to it and see what there is to be seen: that'll fill an hour or two. Then leave the Mansion on your left and climb past the big wood above it (or go through the wood — there are plenty of trails) until you reach the avenue of limes flanking the road from Clifton Lodge Gate. Owls live in these trees; I've seen them; and late on a summer evening the air is busy with bats feeding on bugs. Stroll along the avenue and touch the Lodge, just to be able to say you've walked the Estate from end to end.

AROUND THE MANSION

The House

At 300 feet, Ashton Court is the longest house in Somerset. Or, if there's a longer house, I'd like to see it. The oldest part is in the West Front (on your left as you face it) which probably began as a farmhouse, was enlarged to a manor house, and after the Smyths arrived in 1545 became the start of a very long Mansion. Today, as you stand on the lawn (which itself has been there for a couple of centuries) and look at that tremendous frontage, you're seeing two totally different styles linked by the central gatehouse with its twin turrets. The left wing was built about 1635 in the style of Inigo Jones: very formal and classical for its day. For a long time the right was all stables. About 1810 Sir Hugh Smyth pulled them down and created the balancing wing, plus the stable block on the east side. For a house that was built in stages, over 600 years, it came together very well.

Personally, I think the most attractive part is the oldest: the West Front forms a quiet courtyard with a pair of the biggest and best magnolia trees I know of.

One of the charming things about the Mansion is that it's a bit of a fraud. For all its 300 foot frontage, most of it is only one room deep. So, if you wanted to get (say) from the music room in the right wing to the Long Gallery in the left, you walked nearly all through the house — the length of a football pitch. Twenty-something years ago, I got a guided tour of the whole place, before restoration work began. It was a mess. I remember three things: the roof was very dodgy, the heating system consisted of enormous black radiators, and the butterfly collection took up more space than I lived in.

The Gardens

The Front Lawn is splendid. The secret is simple: roll it and mow it for 200 years. Now you know. To its right (as you face the Mansion) is the Woodland Garden, once a rabbit warren (for meat), now rich with redwoods and cedars. To its left is the Sunken Garden, where the Californian redwoods have begun to do their stuff. The Victorian Smyths planted the seeds; already the trees overtop the house; in 2,000 years they will be up to 360 feet high (storms permitting).

Next is the Rose Garden, and below that a sort of natural amphitheatre, where I once saw Twelfth Night performed. To one side, you can find the Dogs' Graveyard — Lady Esme was very fond of pekes — and the whole length of the grounds is bounded by a ha-ha.

This is a ditch, cleverly dug to separate the garden from the grazing land. Thus the deer couldn't eat the roses but the Smyths could enjoy an unbroken view.

The Deer Park

Until 1939 there were deer all over the Estate: about 300 of them: quite a sight. They all escaped when the place went to pot. A Deer Park was established in 1970 with some fallow deer: smallish, brown or beige with white spots and antlers like fingers. Then came the red deer, much bigger, with antlers like hat-stands.

In January-February, the herd is quiet; the deer are living off their fat. In March or April the stags lose their antlers. By May, most of the females are obviously pregnant. They give birth in June, but don't expect to see it happen — the event is usually hidden by bracken. In July the newborn deer appear in the open. In August-September the stags' antlers are full grown and they scrape off the velvet covering. October sees the rut. Stags do a lot of pacing about in silence; later they bellow; finally they challenge each other. Sometimes the fights lead to injury or death. It's survival of the fittest: only the strongest stags get to breed. In November the herd has to be culled (by shooting or selling) because it grows by as much as a third each year. By December the females are pregnant again, and the deer settle down to survive another winter.

Purdown and Stoke Park

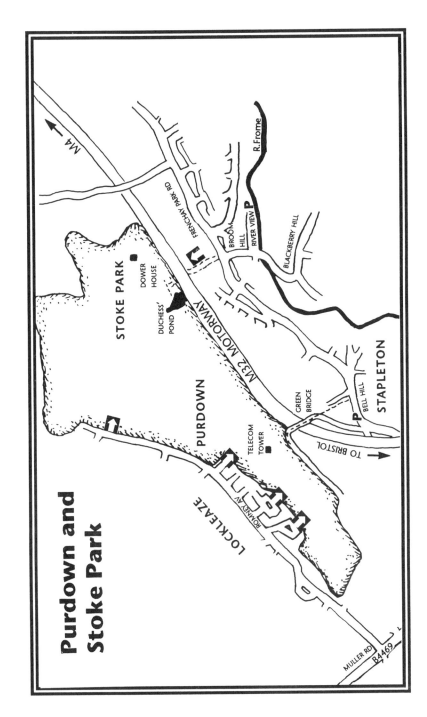

PURDOWN AND STOKE PARK

Many motorists have glanced sideways as they belted along the M32 and said to themselves: 'That looks nice. Wonder how you get to it? Probably private land, anyway.'

Rolling fields, hillsides generously covered with woods, all overlooked by Telecom Tower at one end and a small stately home at the other — yes, it does look nice. The good news is you can easily get to it and no, it isn't privately owned.

In fact, the whole sweep of parkland that most people call Purdown is made up of three sections. The fields and hills beside the M32 are Stoke Park. The long heights are Purdown. Just over the hill near the Tower is half a mile of so-called playing fields; in fact it's good walking space. Each section blends in with the next. Together, they form a walk that's a mile and a quarter long and up to half a mile wide. There are precious few green walks in this quarter of the city, so Purdown is a godsend.

Parking

This depends whether you want to start your walk in Stoke Park from the M32 side, or in Purdown from the Lockleaze side. Lockleaze is the housing estate that runs parallel with Purdown.

Parking on the M32 Side

The obvious entrance to Stoke Park is on the road through Stapleton, where a set of big stone gates still stands.

Starting from the Eastville roundabout under the M32, take

the B4058 north, signposted FRENCHAY and drive for about a mile, past Stapleton church and a Jet garage. At the next mini-roundabout the stone gates are on your left. Turn right into Broom Hill, then left into River View, which leads into a large car-park with 50-60 spaces. Public toilets here. However, this car-park is popular. If it's full, extricate yourself, go back to the mini-roundabout and turn right. Take the second side street, Sheldrake Drive. You're now in a network of a dozen streets where parking is easy.

The only problem is that you're obliged to cross the main road to reach the stone gates into Stoke Park, and it can be a very busy road, with no zebra crossing or even a pedestrian island (at the time of writing). If you have a bunch of wild kids, you might prefer the Green Bridge alternative, which lets you park on the Stoke Park side of the main road.

As before, take the Frenchay road from Eastville roundabout. A couple of hundred yards after the traffic lights, as you go up Bell Hill and pass a little cul-de-sac called Island Gardens on your left, there's a marked parking space for 10-12 cars on the edge of the road, which is wide at this point. Walk up Bell Hill for about 50 yards and find a romantic-looking path running between high walls. This right of way takes you to what I call the Green Bridge over the M32 — it's swathed in green netting. A stile leads into the fields below Telecom Tower.

Alternatively, you could turn off Bell Hill about 50 yards below the parking space I've just described, and go up Heath House Lane, which has signs pointing to Phoenix NHS Trust and Heath House Priory Hospital. This lane leads to the Green Bridge. Drive across it, and you might find a space to park in the bend of the road, if you're lucky.

Parking on the Lockleaze Side

Muller Road runs between Gloucester Road and the

Eastville roundabout. Midway along it, Shaldon Road turns off and soon becomes Romney Avenue - a long, wide street that continues under the brow of the playing fields and Purdown. Not surprisingly, there are plenty of places here where you can park near points of access.

Entering Shaldon Road from Muller Road, after a quarter of a mile (and directly opposite Morris Road) is a wide green path between houses. A little further on there's a similar path between numbers 62 and 64 Romney Avenue. Then Orpen Gardens and Haydon Gardens are cul-de-sacs on the right; each has an exit onto the fields, and opposite Stanfield Close there is a track too. All these points of access get you onto the grass near Telecom Tower.

The next access is a gap between 262 and 270 Romney Avenue. (I don't know where the missing numbers went.) Or you can go to the very end of the Avenue, at numbers 290 and 294, where there are ways in. Plenty of easy parking at all these places.

If you want to walk the full length of Purdown, park near the lower house numbers. If all you want is to see the good looking stretch, park near 262/270 or 290/294. From here you're looking down on Stoke Park, roughly opposite the stone gates at Broom Hill. (You can even drive to the Telecom Tower, but I wouldn't leave my car up there if I were you.)

Finally, you can step straight onto Purdown from Muller Road. Opposite a school playing field, and next to a little cul-de-sac called Elmscroft Crescent, the hillside rises steep and green. Bear off to your right as you climb and you'll come out on a plateau with good views of the city. Now bear left and go alongside the allotments to a stretch of woodland. In its left corner a path through the trees puts you on the track for the Telecom Tower.

The Walks

From the entry at the stone gates, you walk under the M32 and enter Stoke Park. Immediately you see two things: the Duchess' Pond Restoration, a huge piece of landscaping, slap in front of you; and the Dower House, that big building on the hill to your right. More about them later. Notices tell you that you are on Crown Land, and Stay On The Footpath; this isn't difficult because there seem to be footpaths wandering everywhere. One of the notices says 'All poachers will be prosecuted,' so maybe there are partridge and rabbits in the brambles. A metalled road goes left and right but it soon crumbles into pasture — no good for prams but possible for a fairly athletic gran. There may be sheep about. If you have a dog, leave it at home or keep it leashed.

The path to the left leads up to the Telecom Tower. Seen up close, this is an impressive collection of mighty dishes. Stand on the remains of an army camp and you get the best view of Bristol from anywhere in Bristol, plus the long crestline of the Cotswolds heading northwards. Purdown holds its height, so the views as you walk are one of its pleasures.

Alternatively, when you enter the park by the stone gates and under the M32, you can take the path to the right, leading towards the Dower House. (Beyond this are Stoke Park Hospital and the Burden Neurological Institute.) Then follow the track on the left of the House, and look for a flight of steps cut out of the woods on the left again. Go up here (thus avoiding the hospital grounds), cross a stile and turn left up a stony lane. Climb a gate and you're onto the highlands of Purdown. It's easy walking, with clear paths and fine views. Although the Lockleaze estate is only a few hundred yards away, the lie of the land puts it out of sight and out of earshot too.

From here it's a pleasant walk to the Tower and then back down into Stoke Park. The only thing likely to spoil it are motorbikes roaring over Purdown — illegally, deafeningly and dangerously. Tell the police. They'll act, if enough of us ask.

The Dower House

A dower house is where a duke's widow lives. In 1750 the Duke of Beaufort got hold of a mansion that had been built on this site in Elizabethan times, and he turned it into the stately, two-wing, four-floor property you can see, with room space totalling 18,000 square feet. Well, he didn't want his old lady to feel cramped, did he? (Since then, a 15,000 sq.ft. annexe has been added.) Inside, there are what estate agents call 'a number of period features, including ornate cornicing/ceilings, sash windows and period fireplaces.' Outside, there is a splendid view over 400 acres of parkland; Purdown was once the hunting ground of the park. Until recently the Dower House was part of Stoke Park Hospital.

Duchess' Pond

Note the apostrophe. This was the Duchess's Pond. It belonged to her. In the eighteenth century it was fashionable for people with big houses overlooking large estates to pretend they had a river running through the park, even if they didn't. So, in 1768, the Duke had a long, curved lake dug, from the foot of Purdown hill almost as far as the Frome. It covered three and one-third acres, and it looked beautiful until 1968, when the M32 smashed clean through the valley. Duchess' Pond was drained. They took out 63,000 fish.

That included two carp — called Duke and Duchess —

which weighed 23 pounds and 25 pounds; they went to Bristol Zoo.

For a few perilous years there was a real danger that the parkland might be sold for housing. But the people of the Stoke Park Restoration Trust fought the good fight, saved it, and — working with Bristol City Council and with Churngold, the sponsors — they got Duchess' Pond restored, or as much of it as could be fitted in, which is 2.2 acres of lake. The topsoil got stripped off, hundreds of tons of fill were dumped, and the soil was put back. The new pond is the same shape as the old one. Churngold donated enough clay to make a base between two and three metres thick (otherwise the water drains through the bottom). The organisers thought it would take six months to fill the pond; in fact it was filled in just two days. Obviously the Purdown springs are very healthy.

Tree-planting follows the original pattern: oak and hawthorn at the top end, beech and Scots pine at the other. In five or 10 years they'll have matured enough to change the landscape; in 20 years you'll see real woodland. The pond will be full of carp and tench. And the whole parkland will be back to its eighteenth century charm.

Graffiti

The tunnel under the M32 is just a long, unlovely concrete hole, so I can't say that the inevitable rash of graffiti has made it any worse. Two inscriptions stick in my mind. One was rather sad; it said I WISH IT COULD BE CHRISTMAS EVERY DAY. (My idea of purgatory.) The other said KAI IS A CHEESE DOME. Now, was that meant to be insulting or flattering? I think we should be told.

ABBOTTS POOL, FAILAND

This is one of the smallest walks of all, but it has its special charms, and it's very popular.

Directions and Parking

Take the Portishead road (A369) out of Bristol. After Clifton Lodge Gate (entrance to Ashton Court) there are traffic lights. Continue for three quarters of a mile, which takes you to a second set of lights and a pub on your left, The George. Turn left here and drive six-tenths of a mile on a narrow, twisting road with sharp bends, until it stops going down and starts going up. Here, a track crosses the road. Turn right down this track (it has orchards on either side). After 50 yards there is a circular gravelled car-park with room for a couple of dozen cars.

The Walks

There are two ways in. You can follow a level track to the Pool, about a hundred yards further on, or you can climb a log staircase out of the car-park. Take the staircase. This leads you to an interesting variety of twisting trails, through a steep, wooded hillside, and it comes as a pleasant surprise when you find yourself looking down on the Pool. It looks green and mysterious from above. When you climb down to it, it just looks green. It's really a small lake.

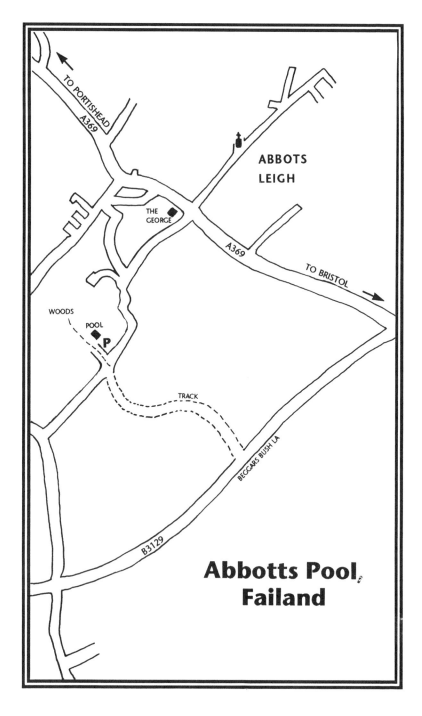

TO PORTISHEAD
A369

ABBOTS
LEIGH

THE
GEORGE

A369

TO BRISTOL

WOODS

POOL

P

TRACK

BEGGARS BUSH LA

B3129

**Abbotts Pool,
Failand**

The whole area divides itself into the wild bit and the tamed bit. On the right hand side of the Pool is pleasant parkland: lots of rhododendrons, some man-made steps, a nice easy stroll. You won't get far, because there isn't far to go. Don't miss the grotto built into the hillside in a far corner of the Pool. At least, I think it's a grotto. Either that or an eighteenth century bus shelter. Very dank and dark inside.

The land on the left is densely wooded. Keep going down the main track, beside the stream, and you'll reach a lane and a farm. Just before this, a fairly rugged path cuts back up into the woods. Trudge up here and eventually it leads you back to the top end of the Pool.

If you feel like more exercise, leave your car in the car-park, go back to the road and follow the path on the opposite side. It'll give you a nice, spacious walk all the way to Beggars Bush Lane — and then back again.

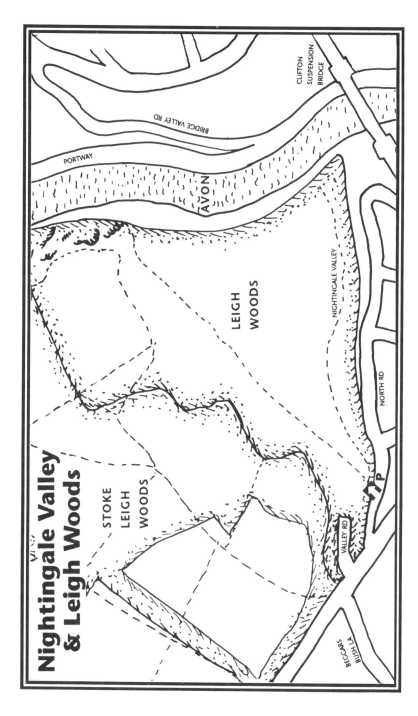

Nightingale Valley & Leigh Woods

STOKE LEIGH WOODS

LEIGH WOODS

NIGHTINGALE VALLEY

AVON

PORTWAY

BRIDGE VALLEY RD

CLIFTON SUSPENSION BRIDGE

NORTH RD

VALLEY RD

BEGGARS BUSH LA

NIGHTINGALE VALLEY
AND LEIGH WOODS

This is the stretch of woods you can see from the Suspension Bridge. Easy to get to, plenty of good paths, lots of lovely trees, and all National Trust. The Valley path is far too rugged for prams and quite a test for grans, but the rest is easy walking.

Parking

There's only one way in at the top, and that's from North Road. Luckily, you can almost always park here, or on Vicarage Road or Church Road, which are nearby. To get there, cross the Suspension Bridge and turn right after about 50 yards. This is North Road. It wanders past huge Victorian houses for a quarter of a mile until — just before it joins the A369 — you see a stile on the right giving entrance to the woods. Alternatively, you can take the A369 up Rownham Hill, past the entrance to Ashton Court, and after a quarter of a mile turn right into North Road, just before the traffic lights.

A Little History

Long before there was a Bristol bridge (and therefore long before there was a Bristol), people were crossing the Avon near Nightingale Valley. The river may look like pure cocoa, but underneath that mud is rock, enough rock to make a ford at low tide. The best ford used to be almost underneath where the Suspension Bridge now is. Ships kept getting stuck on it, and in 1894 it was dynamited to bits. But in the Iron Age — about 650 B.C. to about 50 A.D. — that ford was the M5 of its day. Travellers from the south came down Nightingale Valley, waded the Avon, and went up the defile that came to be called Bridge Valley Road onto the heights of Durdham Down. Naturally, the locals defended this vital route on both sides of the Gorge. On the Clifton side they built a camp above St Vincent's Rocks, where the Observatory now stands; and facing it on the Leigh Woods side they built two camps — Burwalls, near the bridge, hasn't got much left to show for itself, but Stokeleigh, overlooking Nightingale Valley, is still very impressive. A short stroll from the North Road entrance takes you to the walls and ditches protecting Stokeleigh Camp, all seven acres of it. It's unusual in being triangular instead of square. Its great defence, of course, was the Gorge, and there are splendid views to be had, looking out across Bristol.

The Walks

Leigh Woods is generously sprinkled with wide, easy paths. Even on a sunny weekend, you can soon get away from other people; and on a bright winter's day you may well walk for an hour or two without meeting another soul.

Nightingale Valley is easy to find: it runs parallel with North Road. There is no nightingale, the track is steep, stony and narrow, and it takes you exactly where it took the Iron Age travellers — down to the Avon. That means you can either turn around and walk back up, or you can turn right and make a long detour along the tow-path and up Rownham Hill. Some macho types have been known to turn left along the tow-path and find a way back up to Leigh Woods by climbing one of the quarry slopes. I warn you — it may look easy, but it gets tougher the higher you climb, especially when you reach the barbed wire. Definitely not for grans in stiletto heels.

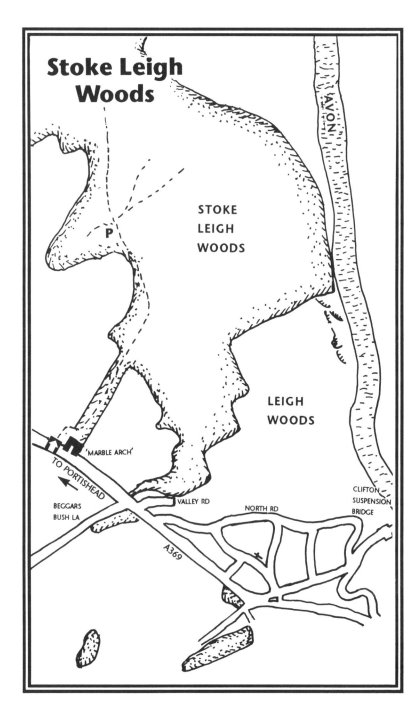

STOKE LEIGH WOODS

This belongs to the Forestry Commission, but it's open to the public, it's big, and it's on the edge of the Avon Gorge.

Directions and Parking

There's only one way in. Take the Portishead road (A369) out of Bristol. Go past Clifton Lodge Gate (entrance to Ashton Court) and cross the traffic lights at Beggars Bush Lane (B3129). Drive on for a quarter of a mile. Watch out for a monument on the right that looks like a small Marble Arch. The entrance is to the left of this arch.

You're now on Forestry Commission land. There's only one road and it take you half a mile to the car-park. This has space for 20 cars or more, but I've never seen more than three in here, and one was occupied by a sales rep reading the *Sun*.

The Walks

Stoke Leigh isn't a timber farm, stocked with boring conifers all planted in rows. Nevertheless, you never know when the professionals with the chains and the chainsaws might turn up and level a chunk of hillside; so I can't promise you it won't be inches deep in mud and small branches at any one particular spot. But Stoke Leigh Woods cover a very wide area and most of it is walkable all year round. The trails are broad and easy. Not suitable for prams, perhaps, although perfectly good for most grans. Keep walking and you're bound to reach the edge of the Avon Gorge. There are some fine views, especially in autumn. Give yourself plenty of time and enjoy getting slightly lost.

Stoke Leigh and Leigh Woods — Forestry Commission and National Trust — fit into each other like two pieces in a jigsaw puzzle. Well-made trails link them, so you can walk into and out of each section. Together, they offer at least a mile of good forest walking from end to end, and a lot more if you criss-cross the woods. All this, only five or ten minutes' drive from Clifton by way of the Suspension Bridge.

BOURTON COMBE, FLAX BOURTON

Strictly speaking, this isn't inside the city, but it's so handy that I chucked it in anyway. Not big — less than a mile long — but full of wild surprise.

Directions and Parking

There's only one way in. Take the Weston-super-Mare road (A370) out of Bristol, to Flax Bourton. The turn-off to Bourton Combe is not conspicuous, so start getting your wits about you when you pass the Jubilee Inn. Soon you'll also pass the junction of the B3129. Now start to slow down. About 200 yards after this junction, a long stone wall on your left suddenly ends where a lane enters from the left. It's marked Bourton Combe, and it's opposite a fire hydrant sign (a big H). If you reach the church, you've gone too far. Drive to the top of the lane. There's not much space, so park intelligently.

The Walks

A path to the right soon leads to a broad, clear track that takes you up the left-hand edge of the woods, past some very old trees indeed. Parts of the Combe look as if they haven't been touched for hundreds of years. Halfway up the

77

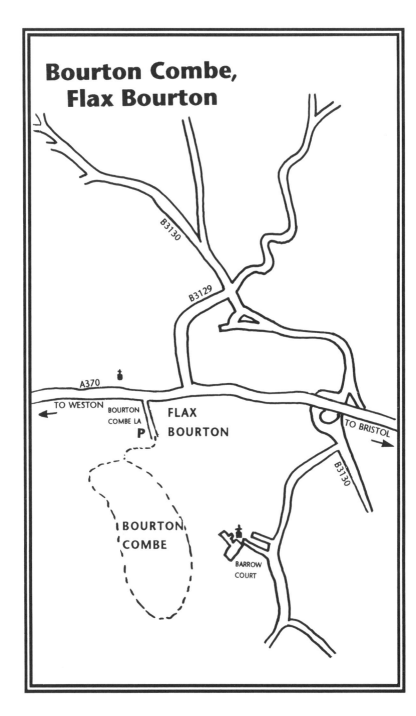

wood, the ground starts to level off and you can cut across to the right, where there is a long, grassy clearing in the forest that looks straight out of a bit of Shakespeare and is just right for a picnic. It overlooks a deep gully. Make your way down into this and it leads through the right hand side of the Combe, getting steeper and more overhung by trees and creepers all the while; at dusk it's pure magic. Eventually you end up where you began.

Alternatively, you can simply follow the first track (up the left hand side of the wood) onwards and upwards, until you emerge onto open farmland. There are some fine, airy views to be had. By following the obvious paths for half a mile or more you can work your way as far as the A38. And then back, I suppose.

Nothing too strenuous about this walk, but it gets a bit rocky underfoot in places. As a change, when you leave the car you could take the path across the fields to the left of Bourton Combe, to Barrow Court.

There's a public footpath to the church but no right of way into the actual Court itself; however, there's nothing to stop you peering at it from a distance. It's a Jacobean house, built on the site of a Benedictine nunnery, and much refurbished about 100 years ago, when the formal gardens were built. You get a good view of these as you pass: lots of obelisks, terraces, balustrades, and a semi-circle of pillars carrying busts that depict the 12 months. A very formal garden indeed.

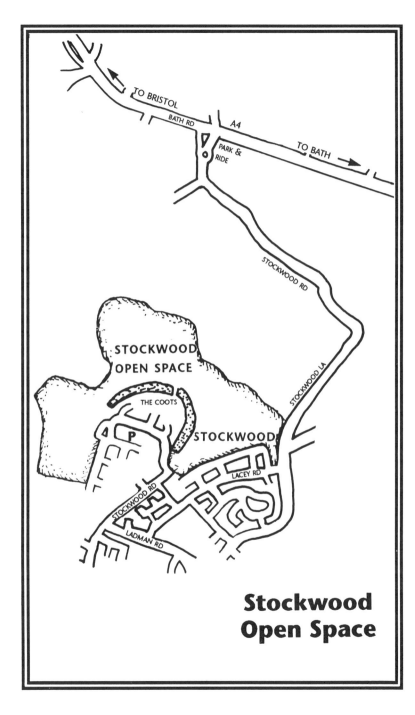

Stockwood
Open Space

STOCKWOOD OPEN SPACE

Stockwood is one of those places that most Bristolians have never been to. It's just a name on the front of a bus. This is not altogether surprising because unless you know how to get there, Stockwood isn't easy to find. It lies somewhere between Whitchurch (on the Wells Road) and Brislington (on the Bath Road). Stockwood is, in fact, the last housing estate in south-east Bristol before you hit Wansdyke and the green belt that keeps Keynsham at bay. So now you know.

How to Get There

The street you're looking for is called The Coots. It forms a semicircle around which the Open Space fits like an enormous hat. Anyone who lives in Stockwood knows where The Coots is (or are). If you're coming from Bristol, take the Bath Road (A4) to Brislington. Turn right at the big crossroads beside the Park & Ride, into Stockwood Road, which becomes Stockwood Lane. Watch out — it twists a lot, and some twists are narrow. Drive to the end (about a mile), turn right at the T-junction and turn right again into Lacey Road. Drive to the end, turn right yet again, and where the road bends sharply to the left, The Coots begins. You can park in a lay-by on the corner, or in one of several cul-de-sacs that make up The Coots.

Alternatively, take the Wells Road (A57) to Whitchurch, turn left into Staunton Road, left again into Stockwood

Lane, and finally left into Stockwood Road, which goes all through Stockwood and ends at The Coots.

The Walk

On the city side of Stockwood is its Open Space, sixty acres of abandoned farmland, a lot of which has been allowed to go back to trees. There's nothing wildly exciting here, no raging rivers or echoing gorges. What the space mainly consists of is woodland and grass. But any kind of wild land is scarce on this side of Bristol, so the Stockwood Open Space is doubly valuable. What's more, it's on a slope — part of Dundry Hill, in fact — which gives long and interesting views of more greenery in the foreground (Knowle golf course; various playing fields) and of the city beyond. When the wind's in the right direction you can see Clifton Suspension Bridge.

If you walk all around the Space you'll cover about one and a half miles. To be honest, it's a bit scruffy in parts, mainly because the locals use it to dump their scrap, but the wild birds don't seem to care; they are many and they sing their little hearts out — everything from wrens to willow warblers and from finches to cuckoos, plus some less outspoken birds, such as little owls and kestrels. There's a circular tarmac path that can be useful to walkers — the ground soon gets very mucky when it rains — and there are dozens of tracks through the trees too.